Learning
AngularJS

Addison-Wesley Learning Series

LEARNING jQuery
A Hands-on Guide to Building Rich Interactive Web Frontends
RALPH STEYER

LEARNING iOS DEVELOPMENT
A Hands-on Guide to the Fundamentals of iOS Programming
MAURICE SHARP
ERICA SADUN
ROD STROUGO

LEARNING Node.js
A Hands-On Guide to Building Web Applications in JavaScript
MARC WANDSCHNEIDER

LEARNING Android Application PROGRAMMING
A Hands-on Guide to Building Android Applications
JAMES TALBOT
JUSTIN McLEAN

Visit **informit.com/learningseries** for a complete list of available publications.

The **Addison-Wesley Learning Series** is a collection of hands-on programming guides that help you quickly learn a new technology or language so you can apply what you've learned right away.

Each title comes with sample code for the application or applications built in the text. This code is fully annotated and can be reused in your own projects with no strings attached. Many chapters end with a series of exercises to encourage you to reexamine what you have just learned, and to tweak or adjust the code as a way of learning.

Titles in this series take a simple approach: they get you going right away and leave you with the ability to walk off and build your own application and apply the language or technology to whatever you are working on.

◆◆Addison-Wesley **informIT** the trusted technology learning source | Safari Books Online

PEARSO

Learning
AngularJS

Brad Dayley

✦✦Addison-Wesley

Upper Saddle River, NJ • Boston • Indianapolis • San Francisco
New York • Toronto • Montreal • London • Munich • Paris • Madrid
Cape Town • Sydney • Tokyo • Singapore • Mexico City

Learning AngularJS

ISBN-13: 978-0-134-03454-6
ISBN-10: 0-134-03454-6

Library of Congress Control Number: 2014951593

Printed in the United States of America

First Printing: December 2014

Trademarks

All terms mentioned in this book that are known to be trademarks or service marks have been appropriately capitalized. The publisher cannot attest to the accuracy of this information. Use of a term in this book should not be regarded as affecting the validity of any trademark or service mark.

Warning and Disclaimer

Every effort has been made to make this book as complete and as accurate as possible, but no warranty or fitness is implied. The information provided is on an "as is" basis. The author and the publisher shall have neither liability nor responsibility to any person or entity with respect to any loss or damages arising from the information contained in this book.

Special Sales

For information about buying this title in bulk quantities, or for special sales opportunities (which may include electronic versions; custom cover designs; and content particular to your business, training goals, marketing focus, or branding interests), please contact our corporate sales department at corpsales@pearsoned.com or (800) 382-3419.

For government sales inquiries, please contact governmentsales@pearsoned.com.

For questions about sales outside the U.S., please contact international@pearsoned.com.

Acquisitions Editor
Mark Taber

Managing Editor
Kristy Hart

Project Editor
Elaine Wiley

Copy Editor
Cheri Clark

Senior Indexer
Cheryl Lenser

Proofreader
Katie Matejka

Technical Editor
Jesse Smith

Editorial Assistant
Vanessa Evans

Designer
Chuti Prasertsith

Senior Compositor
Gloria Schurick

Contents at a Glance

Table of Contents

About the Author

Brad Dayley is a senior software engineer with over 20 years of experience developing enterprise applications and Web interfaces. He has a passion for new technologies, especially ones that really make a difference in the software industry. He has used JavaScript, jQuery, and AngularJS for years and is the author of *Node.js, MongoDB and AngularJS Web Development, jQuery and JavaScript Phrasebook,* and *Teach Yourself jQuery and JavaScript in 24 Hours.* He has designed and implemented a wide array of applications and services from application servers to complex 2.0 web interfaces. He is also the author of *Teach Yourself MongoDB in 24 Hours, Python Developer's Phrasebook,* and *Teach Yourself Django in 24 Hours.*

Dedication

❖

For D!

A & F

❖

Acknowledgments

I'd like to take this page to thank all those who made this title possible. First, I thank my wonderful wife for the inspiration, love, and support she gives me. I'd never make it far without you. I also want to thank my boys for the help they are when I am writing. Thanks to Mark Taber for getting this title rolling in the right direction, Cheri Clark and Katie Matejka for helping me turn technical ramblings into readable text, Jesse Smith for keeping me clear and technically accurate, and Elaine Wiley for managing the project and making sure the final book is the finest quality.

We Want to Hear from You!

As the reader of this book, *you* are our most important critic and commentator. We value your opinion and want to know what we're doing right, what we could do better, what areas you'd like to see us publish in, and any other words of wisdom you're willing to pass our way.

We welcome your comments. You can email or write directly to let us know what you did or didn't like about this book—as well as what we can do to make our books better.

Please note that we cannot help you with technical problems related to the topic of this book, and that due to the high volume of mail we receive, we might not be able to reply to every message.

When you write, please be sure to include this book's title and author, as well as your name and phone or email address.

Email: feedback@developers-library.info

Mail: Reader Feedback
Addison-Wesley Developer's Library
800 East 96th Street
Indianapolis, IN 46240 USA

Reader Services

Visit our website and register this book at **www.informit.com/register** for convenient access to any updates, downloads, or errata that might be available for this book.

Introduction

Welcome to *Learning AngularJS*. This book is designed to catapult you into the world of using AngularJS to build highly interactive yet well-structured web applications. The book covers the basics of the AngularJS framework and how to use it to build well-designed, reusable components for web applications. AngularJS is one of the most exciting and innovative technologies emerging in the world of web development.

This introduction covers the following:

- Who should read this book
- Why you should read this book
- What you will be able to achieve using this book
- What AngularJS is and why it is a great technology
- How this book is organized
- Where to find the code examples

Let's get started.

Who Should Read This Book

This book is aimed at readers who already have an understanding of the basics of HTML and have done some programming in a modern programming language. Having an understanding of JavaScript and jQuery will make this book easier to digest, but is not required as the basics of JavaScript are covered.

Why You Should Read This Book

This book will teach you how to create powerful, interactive web applications that have a well-structured, easy-to-reuse code base that will be easy to maintain. A great feature about

AngularJS is that it actually forces you to become a better web developer by adhering to the underlying structure and design.

The typical readers of this book want to master AngularJS for the purpose of building highly interactive web applications. The typical reader will also want to leverage the innovative MVC approach of AngularJS to implement well-designed and structured web pages and web applications. Overall, AngularJS provides an easy-to-implement, fully integrated web development platform enabling you to implement amazing Web 2.0 applications.

What You Will Learn from This Book

Reading this book will enable you to build real-world, dynamic websites and web applications. Websites are no longer simple static content that consist of HTML pages with integrated images and formatted text. Instead, websites have become much more dynamic, with a single page often serving as the entire site or application.

Using AngularJS technology enables you to build logic directly into your web page that binds the data model for the client web application to back-end services and databases. AngularJS also enables you to easily extend the capability of HTML so that the UI design logic can be expressed easily in an HTML template file. Following are just a few of the things you will learn while reading this book:

- How to quickly build AngularJS templates with built-in directives that enhance the user experience
- How to bind UI elements to the data model so that when the model changes the UI changes and vice versa
- How to bind mouse and keyboard events directly to the data model and back-end functionality to provide robust user interactions
- How to define your own custom AngularJS directives that extend the HTML language
- How to implement client-side services that can interact with the web server
- How to build dynamic browser views that provide rich user interaction
- How to create custom services that can easily be reused in other AngularJS applications
- How to implement rich UI components such as zoomable images and expandable lists as custom AngularJS directives

What Is AngularJS?

AngularJS is a client-side framework developed by Google. It is written in JavaScript with a reduced jQuery library called jQuery lite. The entire ideology behind AngularJS is to provide a framework that makes it easy to implement well-designed and well-structured web pages and applications using an MVC framework.

AngularJS provides all that functionality to handle user input in the browser, manipulate data on the client side, and control how elements are displayed in the browser view. Here are some of the benefits AngularJS provides:

- **Data Binding:** AngularJS has a very clean method to bind data to HTML elements using its powerful scope mechanism.

- **Extensibility:** The AngularJS architecture enables you to easily extend almost every aspect of the language to provide your own custom implementations.

- **Clean:** AngularJS forces you to write clean, logical code.

- **Reusable Code:** The combination of extensibility and clean code makes it very easy to write reusable code in AngularJS. In fact, the language often forces you to do so when you're creating custom services.

- **Support:** Google is investing a lot into this project, which gives it an advantage where other similar initiatives have failed.

- **Compatibility:** AngularJS is based on JavaScript and has a close relationship with jQuery. That makes it easier to begin integrating AngularJS into your environment and reuse pieces of your existing code within the structure of the AngularJS framework.

How Is This Book Organized?

This book is divided into 11 chapters and one appendix:

Chapter 1, "Jumping into JavaScript," provides sort of a JavaScript primer just in case you are not familiar with JavaScript. This chapter also walks you through the process of setting up a development environment with a Node.js server that you can use to follow along with some of the examples. You should at least check out the first few sections even if you are familiar with JavaScript so that you can create the development environment.

Chapter 2, "Getting Started with AngularJS," covers the basics of the AngularJS framework. You will learn how AngularJS is organized and how to design AngularJS applications.

Chapter 3, "Understanding AngularJS Application Dynamics," covers the basic structure of an AngularJS application. You will learn how to define modules and how dependency injection works in AngularJS.

Chapter 4, "Implementing the Scope as a Data Model," covers the relationship between the data model in AngularJS called the scope and other AngularJS components. You also will learn how scope hierarchy works.

Chapter 5, "Using AngularJS Templates to Create Views," covers the structure of AngularJS templates. You will learn how to add elements to the template that reflect data in the model and how to use filters to automatically format elements as they are rendered to the browser view.

Chapter 6, "Implementing Directives in AngularJS Views," covers the built-in AngularJS directives. You will learn how to implement directives in various ways, from turning a simple JavaScript array into multiple HTML elements to binding elements on the web page directly to the scope model. You'll also learn how to handle mouse and keyboard events in the controller.

Chapter 7, "Creating Your Own Custom Directives to Extend HTML," covers creating custom AngularJS directives. You'll learn how to build directives that can enhance the behavior of existing HTML elements as well as create completely new HTML elements that provide great interactions for users.

Chapter 8, "Using Events to Interact with Data in the Model," covers the types of events you will encounter and how to manage them. You will learn how to create and handle your own custom events. This chapter also covers watching values in the scope model and taking action when they change.

Chapter 9, "Implementing AngularJS Services in Web Applications," covers the built-in services that AngularJS provides. These services enable you to communicate with the web server using HTTP requests, interact with the browser, and implement animation of elements on the web page.

Chapter 10, "Creating Your Own Custom AngularJS Services," covers the mechanics available in AngularJS to create your own custom services. Custom services are a great way to make functionality reusable because you can easily inject the functionality provided by custom services into multiple applications.

Chapter 11, "Creating Rich Web Application Components the AngularJS Way," covers using AngularJS mechanisms to build richly interactive page elements. This chapter kind of acts as a review of all the others. You will learn about how to build expandable/collapsible elements, drag and drop functionality, zoomable images, tabbed panels, and star ratings using AngularJS.

Appendix A, "Testing AngularJS Applications," discusses unit and end-to-end testing in AngularJS. This appendix provides some simple pointers for when you're designing tests and also some links to additional resources.

Getting the Code Examples

Throughout this book you will find code examples contained in listing blocks. The titles for the listing blocks include a filename of the file that contains the source. You can access the source-code files and images used in the examples on GitHub.

Finally

I hope you enjoy this book and enjoy learning about AngularJS as much I did. It is a great, innovative technology that is really fun to use. Soon you'll be able to join the many other web developers who use AngularJS to build interactive websites and web applications.

Jumping Into JavaScript

AngularJS relies on JavaScript and a light version of jQuery to provide client-side application logic. Therefore, you need at least a basic understanding of JavaScript before you can jump into the AngularJS world. This chapter has two purposes: helping you set up a development environment and helping you understand the basics of the JavaScript language.

The first part of this chapter discusses the necessary basics of setting up a JavaScript development environment. You should at least take a quick look at this section even if you already are familiar with JavaScript and have a development environment set up. This section discusses using Node.js for the environment, which is important in later chapters where Node.js is used to provide server-side scripting.

The rest of this chapter is to familiarize you with some of the language basics of JavaScript, such as variables, functions, and objects. It is intended not as a full language guide but rather as a synopsis of important syntax and idioms. If you are not familiar with JavaScript, working through this primer should enable you to understand the examples throughout the rest of the book. If you already know JavaScript well, you can either skip those sections or review them as a refresher.

Setting Up a JavaScript Development Environment Using Node.js

There are so many methods for setting up a JavaScript development environment that it is difficult to focus on just one. Most good Integrated Development Environment (IDE) tools provide at least some sort of capability to easily set up a JavaScript development environment. So if you have a favorite IDE, you should check out what JavaScript capabilities it has.

To effectively work with JavaScript to build AngularJS applications, your development environment needs to have the following components:

- **Editor:** The editor is simply there to enable you to create the necessary JavaScript, HTML, and CSS files to build your AngularJS application. There are many editors out there, so pick one you are familiar with. I typically use Eclipse because it tends to have all the functionality I need.

- **Web Server:** The web server will need the capability to serve the static HTML, CSS, and JavaScript files as well as the capability to provide at least some server-side scripting to handle HTTP requests from the AngularJS applications. For most basic setups you can simply have the web server running on your development machine.

- **Browser:** The final component you will need is a web browser to test and try your applications. For the most part JavaScript and AngularJS applications will run across the major browsers the same. However, there is also some functionality that will not work the same between browsers. It is always a good idea to test your applications in the major browsers that your customers will use to ensure that it works correctly in all of them.

To set up your development environment, first pick your favorite editor that supports JavaScript, HTML, and CSS. Then choose a good web browser. For this book, I've used Eclipse and Chrome as my editor and browser (however, the examples also work in Firefox and newer versions of Internet Explorer).

Finally, you need to set up a web server. I thought about using something like XAMPP that provides an Apache web server, or focusing on a specific IDE's capabilities, but instead decided to go with Node.js using Express. I made that choice for several reasons. The first reason is that Node.js is just cool and I think everyone who does JavaScript development should at least look at it. The second reason is that Node.js is very easy to set up and get running, as you will see in a moment. The third reason is that for first learning JavaScript, Node.js is much simpler to use than having to deal with using a web server and browser.

Setting Up Node.js

Node.js is a JavaScript platform based on Google Chrome's V8 engine that enables you to run JavaScript applications outside of a web browser. It is an extremely powerful tool, but in this book I'm going to cover only the basics of using it as the web server to support the AngularJS application examples.

To install and use Node.js you will need to perform the following steps:

1. Go out to the following URL and click on "INSTALL." This will download an installable package to your system. For Windows boxes you will get a .MSI file, for Macs you will get a .PKG file, and for Linux boxes you can get a .tar.gz file.

   http://nodejs.org

2. Install the package. For Windows and Macs simply install the package file. For Linux go out to the following location for instructions on installing using a package manager.

   https://github.com/joyent/node/wiki/Installing-Node.js-via-package-manager

3. Open a terminal or console window.

4. Type node to launch the Node.js JavaScript shell and you should see a > prompt. The Node.js shell provides the capability to execute JavaScript commands directly on the underlying JavaScript engine.

5. If the node application is not found, you need to add the path to the node binary directory to the PATH for your development system (this process is different for each different platform). The binary directory is typically /usr/local/bin/ on Macs and Linux boxes. On Windows the binary directory will be in the <install>/bin folder where <install> is the location you specified during the install process.

6. Then you get to the > prompt. Type the following command and verify that Hello is printed on the screen:

```
console.log("Hello");
```

7. Use the following command to exit the Node.js prompt:

```
process.exit();
```

You have now successfully installed and configured Node.js.

Using Node.js to Run JavaScript

One of the things that I love about Node.js is how easy it is to run and test JavaScript code. This speeds up development by enabling you to easily test functions and snippets without a web browser or web server. There are two main methods to run JavaScript code using Node.js.

The first method to run JavaScript using Node.js is to simply type the JavaScript code directly in the Node.js shell. This is the method you used in the preceding section where you printed Hello on the screen. One thing to note is that when you execute commands in the Node.js shell, the result of those commands is also displayed along with the output. If the statement being executed does not return a result, then the word undefined is displayed. That is why you saw an undefined also printed after the Hello.

The second method to run JavaScript using Node.js is to create a JavaScript file and then execute it from the console prompt. For example, you can also create a file named hello.js with the following contents:

```
console.log("Hello");
```

Then you can run that JavaScript file from the console prompt using the following command:

```
node hello.js
```

This assumes that hello.js is in the current location in the console. If the JavaScript file is in another location, you will need to specify the path to that file. For example:

```
node path_to_file/hello.js
```

The final method to run JavaScript using Node.js is to use the require() method either from the Node.js shell or in a JavaScript file that is being executed from the command line. The require() method will load and execute a JavaScript file. This enables you to import functionality from the external JavaScript file. For example:

```
require("path_tofile/hello.js");
```

Creating an Express Web Server Using Node.js

The best way to use Node.js as the web server for your AngularJS development is to utilize the Express module. Node.js is a very modular platform, meaning that Node.js itself provides a very efficient and extensible framework and external modules are utilized for much of the needed functionality. Consequently, Node.js provides a very nice interface to add and manage these external modules.

Express is one of these modules. The Express module provides a simple-to-implement web server with a robust feature set, such as static files, routes, cookies, request parsing, and error handling.

The simplest way to explain Node.js modules and Express is to simply have you build your own web server using Node.js and Eclipse. In the following exercise you will build a Node.js/Express web server and use it to serve static HTML, CSS, and image files. This should familiarize you with the basics necessary for you to complete the rest of the examples throughout this book.

> **Note**
>
> The images and code files for this and all the examples throughout this book can be downloaded from the code archive on Github.

Use the following steps to build and test a Node.js/Express web server capable of supporting static files and server-side scripting:

1. Create a project folder that you will be using for the examples in this book.

2. From a console prompt, navigate to that project folder and execute the following command. This command will install the Express module version 4.6.1 for Node.js into a subfolder named `node_modules`:

   ```
   npm install express@4.6.1
   ```

3. Now execute the following command to install the body-parser module for Node.js. This module makes it possible to parse the query parameters and body from HTTP GET and POST requests. This command will install the boyd-parser module version 1.6.5 for Node.js into a subfolder named `node_modules`:

   ```
   npm install body-parser@1.6.5
   ```

4. Create a file named `server.js` in the root of your project directory, place the contents from Listing 1.1 inside of it, and save it.

5. Create an HTML file named `ch01/welcome.html` in the project area, place the contents from Listing 1.2 inside it, and then save the file.

6. Create a file named `ch01/css/welcome.css` in your project area, place the contents of Listing 1.3 inside it, and save the file.

7. Copy the `welcome.png` file from the `/images` folder in this book's code archive to the location `images/welcome.png` in your project area or substitute your own file named `welcome.png`.

8. From a console prompt in the project folder, start the Node.js/Express server using the following command:

```
node server.js
```

9. Hit the server from a web browser at the following address. The resulting web page is shown in Figure 1.1.

```
localhost/ch01/welcome.html
```

Listing 1.1 **`server.js`: Creating a Basic Node.js/Express Web Server**

```
01 var express = require('express');
02 var app = express();
03 app.use('/', express.static('./'));
04 app.listen(80);
```

Listing 1.2 **`welcome.html`: Implementing a Welcome Web Page to Test the Node.js/ Express Web Server**

```
01 <!DOCTYPE html>
02 <html>
03   <head>
04     <title>Welcome</title>
05     <link rel="stylesheet" type="text/css" href="css/welcome.css">
06   </head>
07   <body>
08     <img src="images/welcome.png">
09     <p>Welcome to Learning AngularJS. Over the course of
10        of this book you will get a chance to delve into
11        the basics of building AngularJS applications. Enjoy!</p>
12   </body>
13 </html>
```

Listing 1.3 **`welcome.css`: Adding a Static CSS File for the Welcome Web Page**

```
01 p {
02     color: red;
03   border: 3px ridge blue;
04   padding: 10px;
05 . width: 600px; }
06 img {
07     width: 600px; }
```

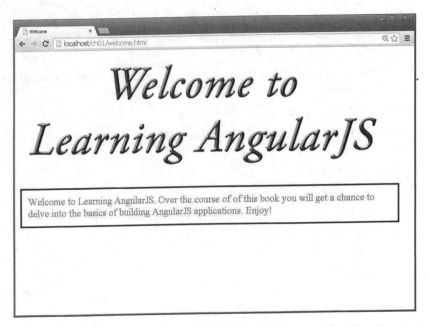

Figure 1.1   Loading static files from a Node.js/Express web server in a browser.

So far you have implemented a basic Node.js/Express web server, created static content, and then loaded the static content from a browser. That is the majority of the necessary capability needed to develop and test your AngularJS applications. There is much, much more to Node.js and Express, and there are capabilities that are not covered in this book because they really fall outside the intended scope of the book. If you are interested learning more about Node.js and Express, I'd suggest looking at the *Node.js, MongoDB and AngularJS Web Development* book.

At this point you have two options. If you are a JavaScript guru, you can skip the rest of this chapter because it only goes over some of the basics of the JavaScript language. If you are not familiar with JavaScript, keep reading and welcome to JavaScript.

Defining Variables

You use variables in JavaScript to temporarily store and access data from your JavaScript files. Variables can point to primitive object types such as numbers or strings, or they can point to more complex objects such as arrays.

To define a variable in JavaScript, you use the `var` keyword and then give the variable a name, as in this example:

```
var myData;
```

You can also assign a value to the variable in the same line. For example, the following line of code creates a variable `myString` and assigns it the value `"Some Text"`:

```
var myString = "Some Text";
```

This single line does the same thing as the following two lines:

```
var myString;
myString = "Some Text";
```

After you have declared a variable, you can use its name to assign a value to the variable and access the value of the variable. For example, the following code stores a string into the `myString` variable and then uses it when assigning the value to the `newString` variable:

```
var myString = "Some Text";
var newString = myString + " Some More Text";
```

You should give variables descriptive names so that you know later what data they store and can more easily use them in your programs. A variable name must begin with a letter, $, or _, and it cannot contain spaces. In addition, variable names are case sensitive, so `myString` is different from `MyString`.

Understanding JavaScript Data Types

JavaScript uses data types to determine how to handle data that is assigned to a variable. The variable type determines what operations you can perform on the variable, such as looping or executing. The following list describes the types of variables that you will most commonly work with in this book:

- **String:** This data type stores character data as a string. The character data is specified by either single or double quotes. All the data contained in the quotes will be assigned to the string variable. For example:

  ```
  var myString = 'Some Text';
  var anotherString = 'Some More Text';
  ```

- **Number:** This data type stores the data as a numerical value. Numbers are useful in counting, calculations, and comparisons. Here are some examples:

  ```
  var myInteger = 1;
  var cost = 1.33;
  ```

- **Boolean:** This data type stores a single bit that is either true or false. Booleans are often used for flags. For example, you might set a variable to `false` at the beginning of some code and then check it on completion so see whether the code execution hit a certain spot. The following examples define `true` and `false` variables:

  ```
  var yes = true;
  var no = false;
  ```

- **Array:** An indexed array is a series of separate distinct data items, all stored under a single variable name. Items in the array can be accessed by their zero-based index, using `array[index]`. The following is an example of creating a simple array and then accessing the first element, which is at index 0:

```
var arr = ["one", "two", "three"];
var first = arr[0];
```

- **Object Literal:** JavaScript supports the capability to create and use object literals which are similar to Dictionaries in Java, C#, and Python. When you use an object literal, you can access values and functions in the object by using `object.property` syntax. The following example shows how to create and access properties of an object literal:

```
var obj = {"name": "Brad", "occupation": "Hacker", "age": "Unknown"};
var name = obj.name;
```

- **Null:** Sometimes you do not have a value to store in a variable either because it hasn't been created or you are no longer using it. At such a time you can set a variable to `null`. Using `null` is better than assigning a value of 0 or an empty string (`""`) because those might be valid values for the variable. By assigning `null` to a variable, you can assign no value and check against `null` inside your code, like this:

```
var newVar = null;
```

Note

JavaScript is a typeless language. You do not need to specify in the script what data type a variable is. The interpreter automatically figures out the correct data type for a variable. In addition, you can assign a variable of one type to a value of a different type. For example, the following code defines a string variable and then assigns it to an integer value type:

```
var id = "testID";
id = 1;
```

Using Operators

JavaScript operators enable you to alter the value of a variable. You are already familiar with the = operator used to assign values to variables. JavaScript provides several operators that fall into two categories: arithmetic and assignment operators.

Arithmetic Operators

You use arithmetic operators to perform operations between variable and direct values. Table 1.1 shows a list of the arithmetic operations, along with the results that are applied.

Table 1.1   **JavaScript's Arithmetic Operators, with Results Based on y=4 Initially**

Operator	Description	Example	Resulting x
+	Addition	`x=y+5`	9
		`x=y+"5"`	`"45"`
		`x="Four"+y+"4"`	`"Four44"`
-	Subtraction	`x=y-2`	2
++	Increment	`x=y++`	4
		`x=++y`	5
--	Decrement	`x=y--`	4
		`x=--y`	3
*	Multiplication	`x=y*4`	16
/	Division	`x=10/y`	2.5
%	Modulo (remainder of division)	`x=y%3`	1

> **Note**
>
> You can also use the + operator to add strings or to add strings and numbers together. It enables you to quickly concatenate strings as well as add numerical data to output strings. Table 1.1 shows that when you add a numerical value and a string value, the numerical value is converted to a string and then the two strings are concatenated.

Assignment Operators

You use an assignment operator to assign a value to a variable. In addition to the = operator, there are several forms that enable you to manipulate the data as you assign a value. Table 1.2 shows a list of the assignment operations, along with the results that are applied.

Table 1.2   **JavaScript's Assignment Operators, with Results Based on x=10 Initially**

Operator	Example	Equivalent Arithmetic Operators	Resulting x
=	`x=5`	`x=5`	5
+=	`x+=5`	`x=x+5`	15
-=	`x-=5`	`x=x-5`	
*=	`x*=5`	`x=x*5`	
/=	`x/=5`	`x=x/5`	
%=	`x%=5`	`x=x%5`	

Applying Comparison and Conditional Operators

Using conditionals is a way to apply logic to your applications such that certain code will be executed only under the correct conditions. You do this by applying comparison logic to variable values. The following sections describe the comparisons available in JavaScript and how to apply them in conditional statements.

Comparison Operators

A comparison operator evaluates two pieces of data and returns `true` if the evaluation is correct and `false` if the evaluation is not correct. A comparison operator compares the value on the left of the operator against the value on the right.

Table 1.3 shows a list of the comparison operators, along with some examples.

Table 1.3   **JavaScript's Comparison Operators, with Results Based on x=10 Initially**

Operator	Description	Example	Result
==	Equal to (value only)	`x==8`	`false`
		`x==10`	`true`
===	Both value and type are equal	`x===10`	`true`
		`x==="10"`	`false`
!=	Not equal	`x!=5`	`true`
!==	Both value and type are not equal	`x!=="10"`	`true`
		`x!==10`	`false`
>	Greater than	`x>5`	`true`
>=	Greater than or equal to	`x>=10`	`true`
<	Less than	`x<5`	`false`
<=	Less than or equal to	`x<=10`	`true`

You can chain together multiple comparisons by using logical operators and standard parentheses. Table 1.4 shows a list of the logical operators and how to use them to chain together comparisons.

Table 1.4   **JavaScript's Comparison Operators, with Results Based on x=10 and y=5 Initially**

Operator	Description	Example	Result
&&	And	`(x==10 && y==5)`	`true`
		`(x==10 && y>x)`	`false`
	Or	`(x>=10 || y>x)`	`true`

Operator	Description	Example	Result
		`(x<10 && y>x)`	`false`
`!`	Not	`!(x==y)`	`true`
		`!(x>y)`	`false`
	Mix	`(x>=10 && y<x || x==y)`	`true`
		`((x<y || x>=10) && y>=5)`	`true`
		`(!(x==y) && y>=10)`	`false`

Using `if` Statements

An `if` statement enables you to separate code execution based on the evaluation of a comparison. The following lines of code show the conditional operators in `()` and the code to execute if the conditional evaluates to `true` in `{}`:

```
if(x==5){
  do_something();
}
```

In addition to only executing code within the `if` statement block, you can specify an `else` block that will be executed only if the condition is `false`. For example:

```
if(x==5){
  do_something();
} else {
  do_something_else();
}
```

You can also chain together `if` statements. To do this, add a conditional statement along with an `else` statement, as in this example:

```
if(x<5){
  do_something();
} else if(x<10) {
  do_something_else();
} else {
  do_nothing();
}
```

Implementing `switch` Statements

Another type of conditional logic is the `switch` statement. The `switch` statement enables you to evaluate an expression once and then, based on the value, execute one of many different sections of code.

The syntax for the switch statement is as follows:

```
switch(expression){
  case value1:
    <code to execute>
    break;
  case value2:
    <code to execute>
    break;
  default:
    <code to execute if not value1 or value2>
}
```

Here is what happens: The switch statement evaluates the expression entirely and gets a value. The value might be a string, a number, a Boolean, or even an object. The switch expression is then compared to each value specified by the case statement. If the value matches, the code in the case statement is executed. If no values match, the default code is executed.

> **Note**
>
> Typically each case statement includes a break command at the end to signal a break out of the switch statement. If no break is found, code execution continues with the next case statement.

Implementing Looping

Looping is a means to execute the same segment of code multiple times. This is extremely useful when you need to repeatedly perform the same tasks on an array or a set of objects.

JavaScript provides functionality to perform for and while loops. The followings sections describe how to implement loops in JavaScript.

while Loops

The most basic type of looping in JavaScript is the while loop. A while loop tests an expression and continues to execute the code contained in its { } brackets until the expression evaluates to false.

For example, the following while loop executes until i is equal to 5:

```
var i = 1;
while (i<5){
  console.log("Iteration " + i);
  i++;
}
```

This example sends the following output to the console:

```
Iteration 1
Iteration 2
Iteration 3
Iteration 4
```

do/while Loops

Another type of while loop is the do/while loop. This is useful if you always want to execute the code in the loop at least once and the expression cannot be tested until the code has executed at least once.

For example, the following do/while loop executes until days is equal to Wednesday:

```
var days = ["Monday", "Tuesday", "Wednesday", "Thursday", "Friday"];
var i=0;
do{
  var day=days[i++];
  console.log("It's " + day);
} while (day != "Wednesday");
```

This is the output at the console:

```
It's Monday
It's Tuesday
It's Wednesday
```

for Loops

A JavaScript for loop enables you to execute code a specific number of times by using a for statement that combines three statements in a single block of execution. Here's the syntax:

```
for (assignment; condition; update;){
  code to be executed;
}
```

The for statement uses the three statements as detailed here when executing the loop:

- *assignment:* This is executed before the loop begins and not again. It is used to initialize variables that will be used in the loop as conditionals.

- *condition:* This expression is evaluated before each iteration of the loop. If the expression evaluates to true, the loop is executed; otherwise, the for loop execution ends.

- *update:* This is executed on each iteration, after the code in the loop has executed. This is typically used to increment a counter that is used in condition.

The following example illustrates a `for` loop and the nesting of one loop inside another:

```
for (var x=1; x<=3; x++) {
  for (var y=1; y<=3; y++) {
    console.log(x + " X " + y + " = " + (x*y));
  }
}
```

The resulting output to the web console is this:

```
1 X 1 = 1
1 X 2 = 2
1 X 3 = 3
2 X 1 = 2
2 X 2 = 4
2 X 3 = 6
3 X 1 = 3
3 X 2 = 6
3 X 3 = 9
```

for/in Loops

Another type of `for` loop is the `for/in` loop. The `for/in` loop executes on any data type that can be iterated. For the most part, you will use `for/in` loops on arrays and objects. The following example illustrates the syntax and behavior of the `for/in` loop on a simple array:

```
var days = ["Monday", "Tuesday", "Wednesday", "Thursday", "Friday"];
for (var idx in days) {
  console.log("It's " + days[idx] + "<br>");
}
```

Notice that the variable `idx` is adjusted each iteration through the loop, from the beginning array index to the last. This is the resulting output:

```
It's Monday
It's Tuesday
It's Wednesday
It's Thursday
It's Friday
```

Interrupting Loops

When you work with loops, there are times when you need to interrupt the execution of code inside the code itself, without waiting for the next iteration. There are two keywords you can use to do this: `break` and `continue`.

The `break` keyword stops execution of a `for` or `while` loop completely. The `continue` keyword, on the other hand, stops execution of the code inside the loop and continues with the next iteration. Consider the following examples.

This example shows using `break` if the day is Wednesday:

```
var days = ["Monday", "Tuesday", "Wednesday", "Thursday", "Friday"];
for (var idx in days){
  if (days[idx] == "Wednesday")
    break;
  console.log("It's " + days[idx] + "<br>");
}
```

When the value is `Wednesday`, loop execution stops completely:

```
It's Monday
It's Tuesday
```

This example shows using `continue` if the day is Wednesday:

```
var days = ["Monday", "Tuesday", "Wednesday", "Thursday", "Friday"];
for (var idx in days){
  if (days[idx] == "Wednesday")
    continue;
  console.log("It's " + days[idx] + "<br>");
}
```

Notice that the write is not executed for `Wednesday` because of the `continue` statement, but the loop execution does complete:

```
It's Monday
It's Tuesday
It's Thursday
It's Friday
```

Creating Functions

One of the most important parts of JavaScript is making code that other code can reuse. To do this, you organize your code into functions that perform specific tasks. A function is a series of code statements combined in a single block and given a name. You can then execute the code in the block by referencing that name.

Defining Functions

You define a function by using the `function` keyword followed by a name that describes the use of the function, a list of zero or more arguments in `()`, and a block of one or more code statements in `{}`. For example, the following is a function definition that writes `"Hello World"` to the console:

```
function myFunction(){
  console.log("Hello World");
}
```

To execute the code in myFunction(), all you need to do is add the following line to the main JavaScript or inside another function:

```
myFunction();
```

Passing Variables to Functions

Frequently you need to pass specific values to functions, and the functions will use those values when executing their code. You pass values to a function in comma-delimited form. A function definition needs a list of variable names in () that match the number being passed in. For example, the following function accepts two arguments, name and city, and uses them to build the output string:

```
function greeting(name, city){
  console.log("Hello " + name);
  console.log(". How is the weather in " + city);
}
```

To call the greeting() function, you need to pass in a name value and a city value. The value can be a direct value or a previously defined variable. To illustrate this, the following code executes the greeting() function with a name variable and a direct string for city:

```
var name = "Brad";
greeting(name, "Florence");
```

Returning Values from Functions

Often, a function needs to return a value to the calling code. Adding a return keyword followed by a variable or value returns that value from the function. For example, the following code calls a function to format a string, assigns the value returned from the function to a variable, and then writes the value to the console:

```
function formatGreeting(name, city){
  var retStr = "";
  retStr += "Hello <b>" + name + "/n");
  retStr += "Welcome to " + city + "!";
return retStr;
}
var greeting = formatGreeting("Brad", "Rome");
console.log(greeting);
```

You can include more than one `return` statement in the function. When the function encounters a `return` statement, code execution of the function stops immediately. If the `return` statement contains a value to return, that value is returned. The following example shows a function that tests the input and returns immediately if it is zero:

```
function myFunc(value){
  if (value == 0)
    return value;
  <code_to_execute_if_value_nonzero>
  return value;
}
```

Using Anonymous Functions

So far, all the examples you have seen show named functions. JavaScript also lets you create anonymous functions. These functions have the advantage of being defined directly in the parameter sets when you call other functions. Thus you do not need formal definitions.

For example, the following code defines a function `doCalc()` that accepts three parameters. The first two should be numbers, and the third is a function that will be called and passed the two numbers as arguments:

```
function doCalc(num1, num2, calcFunction){
    return calcFunction(num1, num2);
}
```

You could define a function and then pass the function name without parameters to `doCalc()`, as in this example:

```
function addFunc(n1, n2){
    return n1 + n2;
}
doCalc(5, 10, addFunc);
```

However, you also have the option to use an anonymous function directly in the call to `doCalc()`, as shown in these two statements:

```
console.log( doCalc(5, 10, function(n1, n2){ return n1 + n2; }) );
console.log( doCalc(5, 10, function(n1, n2){ return n1 * n2; }) );
```

You can probably see that the advantage of using anonymous functions is that you do not need a formal definition that will not be used anywhere else in your code. Anonymous functions, therefore, make JavaScript code more concise and readable.

Understanding Variable Scope

After you start adding conditions, functions, and loops to your JavaScript applications, you need to understand variable scoping. Variable scoping sets out to determine the value of a specific variable name at the line of code currently being executed.

JavaScript enables you to define both a global version and a local version of a variable. The global version is defined in the main JavaScript, and local versions are defined inside functions. When you define a local version in a function, a new variable is created in memory. Within that function, you reference the local version. Outside that function, you reference the global version.

To understand variable scoping a bit better, consider the code in Listing 1.4.

Listing 1.4   **Defining Global and Local Variables in JavaScript**

```
01 var myVar = 1;
02 function writeIt(){
03   var myVar = 2;
04   console.log("Variable = " + myVar);
05   writeMore();
06 }
07 function writeMore(){
08   console.log("Variable = " + myVar);
09 }
10 writeIt();
```

The global variable `myVar` is defined on line 1, and a local version is defined on line 3, within the `writeIt()` function. Line 4 writes `"Variable = 2"` to the console. Then in line 5, `writeMore()` is called. Since there is no local version of `myVar` defined in `writeMore()`, the value of the global `myVar` is written in line 8.

Using JavaScript Objects

JavaScript has several built-in objects, such as `Number`, `Array`, `String`, `Date`, and `Math`. Each of these built-in objects has member properties and methods. In addition to the JavaScript objects, you will find as you read this book that Node.js, MongoDB, Express, and Angular add their own built-in objects as well.

JavaScript provides a fairly nice object-oriented programming structure for you to create your own custom objects as well. Using objects rather than just a collection of functions is key to writing clean, efficient, reusable JavaScript code.

Using Object Syntax

To use objects in JavaScript effectively, you need to have an understanding of their structure and syntax. An object is really just a container to group together multiple values and, in some instances, functions. The values of an object are called properties and the values of functions are called methods.

To use a JavaScript object, you must first create an instance of the object. You create object instances by using the `new` keyword with the object constructor name. For example, to create a `Number` object, you could use the following line of code:

```
var x = new Number("5");
```

Object syntax is very straightforward: You use the object name and then a dot and then the property or method name. For example, the following lines of code get and set the `name` property of an object named `myObj`:

```
var s = myObj.name;
myObj.name = "New Name";
```

You can also get and set object methods of an object in the same manner. For example, the following lines of code call the `getName()` method and then change the method function on an object named `myObj`:

```
var name = myObj.getName();
myObj.getName = function() { return this.name; };
```

You can also create objects and assign variables and functions directly by using { } syntax. For example, the following code defines a new object and assigns values and a method function:

```
var obj = {
    name: "My Object",
    value: 7,
    getValue: function() { return this.name; };
};
```

You can also access members of a JavaScript object by using the *object[propertyName]* syntax. This is useful when you are using dynamic property names and when the property name must include characters that JavaScript does not support. For example, the following examples access the `"User Name"` and `"Other Name"` properties of an object named `myObj`:

```
var propName = "User Name";
var val1 = myObj[propName];
var val2 = myObj["Other Name"];
```

Creating Custom Defined Objects

As you have seen so far, using the built-in JavaScript objects has several advantages. As you begin to write code that uses more and more data, you will find yourself wanting to build your own custom objects, with specific properties and methods.

You can define JavaScript objects in a couple of ways. The simplest is the on-the-fly method: Simply create a generic object and then add properties to it as needed. For example, to create a user object and assign a first and last name as well as define a function to return them, you could use the following code:

```
var user = new Object();
user.first="Brad";
user.last="Dayley";
user.getName = function( ) { return this.first + " " + this.last; }
```

You could also accomplish the same effect through a direct assignment using the following code, where the object is enclosed in { } and the properties are defined using *property:value* syntax:

```
var user = {
  first: 'Brad',
  last: 'Dayley',
  getName: function( ) { return this.first + " " + this.last; }};
```

These first two options work very well for simple objects that you do not need to reuse later. A better method for reusable objects is to actually enclose an object inside its own function block. This has the advantage of enabling you to keep all the code pertaining to the object local to the object itself. For example:

```
function User(first, last){
  this.first = first;
  this.last = last;
  this.getName = function( ) { return this.first + " " + this.last; };
var user = new User("Brad", "Dayley");
```

The end result of these methods is essentially the same as if you have an object with properties that can be referenced using dot notation, as shown here:

```
console.log(user.getName());
```

Using a Prototyping Object Pattern

An even more advanced method of creating objects is using a prototyping pattern. You implement such a pattern by defining the functions inside the prototype attribute of the object instead of inside the object itself. With prototyping, the functions defined in the prototype are created only once, when the JavaScript is loaded, instead of each time a new object is created.

The following example shows the prototyping syntax:

```
function UserP(first, last){
  this.first = first;
  this.last = last;
}
UserP.prototype = {
  getFullName: function(){
```

```
        return this.first + " " + this.last;
    }
};
```

Notice that you define the object `UserP` and then set `UserP.prototype` to include the `getFullName()` function. You can include as many functions in the prototype as you would like. Each time a new object is created, those functions will be available.

Manipulating Strings

The `String` object is by far the most commonly used object in JavaScript. JavaScript automatically creates a `String` object for you anytime you define a variable that has a string data type. For example:

```
var myStr = "Teach Yourself jQuery & JavaScript in 24 Hours";
```

When you create a string, there are a few special characters that you can't add directly to the string. For those characters, JavaScript provides a set of escape codes, listed in Table 1.5.

Table 1.5 **`String` Object Escape Codes**

Escape	Description	Example	Output String
\'	Single quote mark	"couldn\'t be"	couldn't be
\"	Double quote mark	"I \"think\" I \"am\""	I "think" I "am"
\\	Backslash	"one\\two\\three"	one\two\three
\n	New line	"I am\nI said"	I am I said
\r	Carriage return	"to be\ror not"	to be or not
\t	Tab	"one\ttwo\tthree"	one two three
\b	Backspace	"correctoin\b\b\bion"	correction
\f	Form feed	"Title A\fTitle B"	Title A then Title B

To determine the length of a string, you can use the `length` property of the `String` object, as in this example:

```
var numOfChars = myStr.length;
```

The `String` object has several functions that enable you to access and manipulate the string in various ways. The methods for string manipulation are described in Table 1.6.

Table 1.6   **Methods to Manipulate `String` Objects**

Method	Description
charAt(index)	Returns the character at the specified index.
charCodeAt(index)	Returns the Unicode value of the character at the specified index.
concat(str1, str2, ...)	Joins two or more strings and returns a copy of the joined strings.
fromCharCode()	Converts Unicode values to actual characters.
indexOf(subString)	Returns the position of the first occurrence of a specified subString value. Returns -1 if the substring is not found.
lastIndexOf(subString)	Returns the position of the last occurrence of a specified subString value. Returns -1 if the substring is not found.
match(regex)	Searches the string and returns all matches to the regular expression.
replace(subString/regex, replacementString)	Searches the string for a match of the substring or regular expression and replaces the matched substring with a new substring.
search(regex)	Searches the string, based on the regular expression, and returns the position of the first match.
slice(start, end)	Returns a new string that has the portion of the string between the start and end positions removed.
split(sep, limit)	Splits a string into an array of substrings, based on a separator character or regular expression. The optional limit argument defines the maximum number of splits to make, starting from the beginning.
substr(start,length)	Extracts the characters from a string, beginning at a specified start position, and through the specified length of characters.
substring(from, to)	Returns a substring of characters between the from and to index.
toLowerCase()	Converts the string to lowercase.
toUpperCase()	Converts the string to uppercase.
valueOf()	Returns the primitive string value.

To get you started on using the functionality provided in the `String` object, the following sections describe some of the common tasks that can be done using `String` object methods.

Combining Strings

You can combine multiple strings either by using a + operation or by using the `concat()` function on the first string. For example, in the following code, `sentence1` and `sentence2` will be the same:

```
var word1 = "Today ";
var word2 = "is ";
var word3 = "tomorrow\'s ";
var word4 = "yesterday.";
var sentence1 = word1 + word2 + word3 + word4;
var sentence2 = word1.concat(word2, word3, word4);
```

Searching a String for a Substring

To determine whether a string is a substring of another, you can use the `indexOf()` method. For example, the following code writes the string to the console only if it contains the word think:

```
var myStr = "I think, therefore I am.";
if (myStr.indexOf("think") != -1){
  console.log (myStr);
}
```

Replacing a Word in a String

Another common `String` object task is replacing one substring with another. To replace a word or phrase in a string, you use the `replace()` method. The following code replaces the text `"<username>"` with the value of the variable `username`:

```
var username = "Brad";
var output = "<username> please enter your password: ";
output.replace("<username>", username);
```

Splitting a String into an Array

A very common task with strings is to split them into arrays, using a separator character. For example, the following code splits a time string into an array of its basic parts, using the `split()` method on the `":"` separator:

```
var t = "12:10:36";
var tArr = t.split(":");
var hour = tArr[0];
var minute = tArr[1];
var second = tArr[2];
```

Working with Arrays

The `Array` object provides a means of storing and handling a set of other objects. Arrays can store numbers, strings, or other JavaScript objects. There are a couple of ways to create JavaScript arrays. For example, the following statements create three identical versions of the same array:

```
var arr = ["one", "two", "three"];
var arr2 = new Array();
arr2[0] = "one";
arr2[1] = "two";
arr2[2] = "three";
var arr3 = new Array();
arr3.push("one");
arr3.push("two");
arr3.push("three");
```

The first method defines `arr` and sets the contents in a single statement, using `[]`. The second method creates the `arr2` object and then adds items to it, using direct index assignment. The third method creates the `arr3` object and then uses the best option for extending arrays: It uses the `push()` method to push items onto the array.

To determine the number of elements in an array, you can use the `length` property of the `Array` object, as in this example:

```
var numOfItems = arr.length;
```

Arrays follow a zero-based index, meaning that the first item is at index 0 and so on. For example, in the following code, the value of variable `first` will be `Monday`, and the value of variable `last` will be `Friday`:

```
var week = ["Monday", "Tuesday", "Wednesday", "Thursday", "Friday"];
var first = w [0];
var last = week[week.length-1];
```

The `Array` object has several built-in functions that enable you to access and manipulate arrays in various ways. Table 1.7 describes the methods attached to the `Array` object that enable you to manipulate the array contents.

Table 1.7   **Methods to Manipulate `Array` Objects**

Method	Description
`concat(arr1, arr2, ...)`	Returns a joined copy of the array and the arrays passed as arguments.
`indexOf(value)`	Returns the first index of the value in the array or `-1` if the item is not found.

Method	Description
join(*separator*)	Joins all elements of an array, separated by the separator into a single string. If no separator is specified, a comma is used.
lastIndexOf(*value*)	Returns the last index of the value in the array or -1 if the value is not found.
pop()	Removes the last element from the array and returns that element.
push(*item1*, *item2*, ...)	Adds one or more new elements to the end of an array and returns the new length.
reverse()	Reverses the order of all elements in the array.
shift()	Removes the first element of an array and returns that element.
slice(*start*, *end*)	Returns the elements between the start and end indexes.
sort(*sortFunction*)	Sorts the elements of the array. sortFunction is optional.
splice(*index*, *count*, *item1*, *item2*...)	At the index specified, removes count number items and then inserts at index any optional items passed in as arguments.
toString()	Returns the string form of an array.
unshift()	Adds new elements to the beginning of an array and returns the new length.
valueOf()	Returns the primitive value of an Array object.

To get you started using the functionality provided in the Array object, the following sections describe some of the common tasks that can be done using Array object methods.

Combining Arrays

You can combine arrays into a single array using the concat() method but not the + method. In the following code, the variable arr3 contains a string representation of the elements in arr1 added to a string representation of the elements in arr2. The variable arr4, in the following code, is an array with the combined elements from arr1 and arr2:

```
var arr1 = [1,2,3];
var arr2 = ["three", "four", "five"]
var arr3 = arr1 + arr2;
var arr4 = arr1.concat(arr2);
```

Note

You can combine an array of numbers and an array of strings. Each item in the array will keep its own object type. However, as you use the items in the array, you need to keep track of arrays that have more than one data type so that you do not run into problems.

Iterating Through Arrays

You can iterate through an array by using a `for` or a `for/in` loop. The following code illustrates iterating through each item in the array using each method:

```
var week = ["Monday", "Tuesday", "Wednesday", "Thursday", "Friday"];
for (var i=0; i<week.length; i++){
  console.log("<li>" + week[i] + "</li>");
}
for (dayIndex in week){
  console.log("<li>" + week[dayIndex] + "</li>");
}
```

Converting an Array into a String

A very useful feature of `Array` objects is the capability to combine the elements of a string to make a `String` object, separated by a specific separator using the `join()` method. For example, the following code joins the time components back together into the format `12:10:36`:

```
var timeArr = [12,10,36];
var timeStr = timeArr.join(":");
```

Checking Whether an Array Contains an Item

Often you will need to check whether an array contains a certain item. You can do this by using the `indexOf()` method. If the code does not find the item in the list, it returns a `-1`. The following function writes a message to the console if an item is in the `week` array:

```
function message(day){
  var week = ["Monday", "Tuesday", "Wednesday", "Thursday", "Friday"];
  if (week.indexOf(day) != -1){
    console.log("Happy " + day);
  }
}
```

Adding Items to and Removing Items from Arrays

There are several methods for adding items to and removing items from `Array` objects, using the various built-in methods. Table 1.8 shows some of the various methods used in this book. The values in Table 1.8 are shown in a progression as modified by each consecutive statement.

Table 1.8 **`Array` Object Methods Used to Add Elements to and Remove Elements from Arrays**

Statement	Value of `x`	Value of `arr`
`var arr = [1,2,3,4,5];`	undefined	1,2,3,4,5
`var x = 0;`	0	1,2,3,4,5
`x = arr.unshift("zero");`	6 (length)	zero,1,2,3,4,5
`x = arr.push(6,7,8);`	9 (length)	zero,1,2,3,4,5,6,7,8
`x = arr.shift();`	zero	1,2,3,4,5,6,7,8
`x = arr.pop();`	8	1,2,3,4,5,6,7
`x = arr.splice(3,3,"four","five","six");`	4,5,6	1,2,3,four,five,six,7
`x = arr.splice(3,1);`	four	1,2,3,five,six,7
`x = arr.splice(3);`	five,six,7	1,2,3

Adding Error Handling

An important part of JavaScript coding is adding error handling for instances in which there might be problems. By default, if a code exception occurs because of a problem in your JavaScript, the script fails and does not finish loading. This is not usually the desired behavior. In fact, it is often catastrophic behavior. To prevent these types of big problems, you should wrap your code in a try/catch block.

try/catch Blocks

To prevent your code from totally bombing out, use try/catch blocks that can handle problems inside your code. If JavaScript encounters an error when executing code in a try block, it will jump down and execute the catch portion instead of stopping the entire script. If no error occurs, the whole try block will be executed, and none of the catch block will be executed.

For example, the following try/catch block tries to assign variable x to a value of an undefined variable named badVarName:

```
try{
    var x = badVarName;
} catch (err){
    console.log(err.name + ': "' + err.message +  '" occurred when assigning x.');
}
```

Notice that the catch statement accepts an err parameter, which is an error object. The error object provides the message property, which provides a description of the error. The error object also provides a name property that is the name of the error type that was thrown.

The previous code results in an exception and the following message:

```
ReferenceError: "badVarName is not defined" occurred when assigning x.
```

Throwing Your Own Errors

You can also throw your own errors by using a throw statement. The following code illustrates how to add throw statements to a function to throw an error, even if a script error does not occur. The function sqrRoot() accepts a single argument x. It then tests x to verify that it is a positive number and returns a string with the square root of x. If x is not a positive number, the appropriate error is thrown, and the catch block returns the error:

```
function sqrRoot(x) {
    try {
        if(x=="")     throw {message:"Can't Square Root Nothing"};
        if(isNaN(x)) throw {message:"Can't Square Root Strings"};
        if(x<0)        throw {message:"Sorry No Imagination"};
        return "sqrt("+x+") = " + Math.sqrt(x);
    } catch(err){
        return err.message;
    }
}
function writeIt(){
    console.log(sqrRoot("four"));
    console.log(sqrRoot(""));
    console.log(sqrRoot("4"));
    console.log(sqrRoot("-4"));
}
writeIt();
```

The following is the console output, showing the different errors that are thrown, based on input to the sqrRoot() function:

```
Can't Square Root Strings
Can't Square Root Nothing
sqrt(4) = 2
Sorry No Imagination
```

Using Finally

Another valuable tool in exception handling is the finally keyword. You can add this keyword to the end of a try/catch block. After the try/catch block is executed, the finally block is always executed, whether an error occurs and is caught or the try block is fully executed.

Here's an example of using a `finally` block inside a web page:

```
function testTryCatch(value){
  try {
    if (value < 0){
      throw "too small";
    } else if (value > 10){
      throw "too big";
    }
    your_code_here
  } catch (err) {
    console.log("The number was " + err);
  } finally {
    console.log("This is always written.");
  }
}
```

Summary

Understanding JavaScript is critical to being able to work in the Node.js, MongoDB, Express, and AngularJS environments. This chapter discussed enough of the basic JavaScript language syntax for you to grasp the concepts in the rest of the book. You learned how to create objects, how to use functions, and how to work with strings and arrays. You also learned how to apply error handling to your scripts, which is critical in the Node.js environment.

2

Getting Started with AngularJS

AngularJS is a JavaScript framework that provides a very structured method of creating websites and web applications. Essentially, AngularJS is a JavaScript library that is built on a lightweight version of jQuery—a combination that enables AngularJS to provide the best of JavaScript and jQuery and at the same time enforce a structured Model View Controller (MVC) framework.

AngularJS is a perfect client-side library for most web applications because it provides a very clean and structured approach. With a clean, structured front end, you will find that it is much easier to implement clean, well-structured server-side logic.

This chapter introduces you to AngularJS as well as the major components involved in an AngularJS application. Understanding these components is critical before you try to implement an AngularJS application because the framework is different from more traditional JavaScript web application programming.

After you have a good grasp of the components and the life cycle of an AngularJS application, you'll learn how to construct a basic AngularJS application, step-by-step. This should prepare you to jump into the following chapters, which provide much more detail on implementing AngularJS.

Why AngularJS?

AngularJS is an MVC framework that that is built on top of JavaScript and a lightweight version of jQuery. MVC frameworks separate the business logic in code from the view and the model. Without this separation, JavaScript-based web applications can quickly get out of hand when you are trying to manage all three together and a complex maze of functions.

Everything that AngularJS provides, you could implement yourself by using JavaScript and jQuery, or you could even try using another MVC JavaScript framework. However, AngularJS has a lot of functionality, and the design of the AngularJS framework makes it easy to implement MVC in the correct manner. The following are some of the reasons to choose AngularJS:

- The AngularJS framework forces correct implementation of MVC and also makes it easy to implement MVC correctly.

- The declarative style of AngularJS HTML templates makes the intent of the HTML more intuitive and makes the HTML easier to maintain.

- The model portion of AngularJS is basic JavaScript objects, making it easy to manipulate, access, and implement.

- AngularJS uses a declarative approach to extend the functionality of HTML by having a direct link between the HTML declaratives and the JavaScript functionality behind them.

- AngularJS provides a very simple and flexible filter interface that enables you to easily format data as it passes from the model to the view.

- AngularJS applications tend to use a fraction of the code that traditional JavaScript applications use because you need to focus only on the logic and not all the little details, such as data binding.

- AngularJS requires a lot less Document Object Model (DOM) manipulation than traditional methods and guides you to put the manipulations in the correct locations in applications. It is easier to design applications based on presenting data than on DOM manipulation.

- AngularJS provides several built-in services and enables you to implement your own in a structured and reusable way. This makes your code more maintainable and easier to test.

- Due to the clean separation of responsibilities in the AngularJS framework, it is easy to test your applications and even develop them using a test-driven approach.

Understanding AngularJS

AngularJS provides a very structured framework based on an MVC (Model View Controller) model. This framework enables you to build structured applications that are robust and easily understood and maintained. If you are not familiar with the MVC model, the following paragraph provides a quick synopsis to help you understand the basics. It is by no means complete and only intended to give you enough reference to see how AngularJS applies MVC principles. The Wikipedia website is a great resource if you want additional information about MVC in general.

In MVC, there are three components: the Model is the data source, View is the rendered webpage, and the Controller handles the interaction between the two. A major purpose of MVC is to separate out responsibilities in your JavaScript code to keep it clean and easy to follow. AngularJS is one of the best MVC frameworks available because it makes it very easy to implement MVC.

To get started with AngularJS, you first need to understand the various components that you will be implementing and how they interact with each other. The following sections discuss the various components involved in an AngularJS application, their purpose, and what each is responsible for.

Modules

AngularJS introduces the concept of a module representing components in an application. The module provides a namespace that enables you to reference directives, scopes, and other components based on model name. This makes it easier to package and reuse parts of an application.

Each view or web page in AngularJS has a single module assigned to it via the `ng-app` directive. (Directives are discussed later in this chapter.) However, you can add other modules to the main module as dependencies, which provides a very structured and componentized application. The main AngularJS module acts similar to the root namespace in C# and Java.

Scopes and the Data Model

AngularJS introduces the concept of a scope. A scope is really just a JavaScript representation of data used to populate a view presented on a web page. The data can come from any source, such as a database, a remote web service, or the client-side AngularJS code, or it can be dynamically generated by the web server.

A great feature of scopes is that they are just plain JavaScript objects, which means you can manipulate them as needed in your AngularJS code with ease. Also, you can nest scopes to organize your data to match the context that they are being used in.

Views with Templates and Directives

HTML web pages are based on a DOM in which each HTML element is represented by a DOM object. A web browser reads the properties of a DOM object and knows how to render the HTML element on the web page, based on the DOM object's properties.

Most dynamic web applications use direct JavaScript or a JavaScript-based library such as jQuery to manipulate a DOM object to change the behavior and appearance of the rendered HTML element in the user view.

AngularJS introduces a new concept of combining templates that contain directives which extend the HTML tags and attributes directly with JavaScript code in the background to extend the capability of HTML. Directives have two parts. The first part is extra attributes, elements, and CSS classes that are added to an HTML template. The second part is JavaScript code that extends the normal behavior of the DOM.

The advantage of using directives is that the intended logic for visual elements is indicated by the HTML template such that it is easy to follow and is not hidden within a mass of JavaScript code. One of the best features of AngularJS is that the built-in AngularJS directives handle most of the necessary DOM manipulation functionality that you need in order to bind the data in the scope directly to the HTML elements in the view.

You can also create your own AngularJS directives to implement any necessary custom functionality you need in a web application. In fact, you should use your own custom directives to do any direct DOM manipulation that a web application needs.

Expressions

A great feature of AngularJS is the capability to add expressions inside the HTML template. AngularJS evaluates expressions and then dynamically adds the result to a web page. Because expressions are linked to the scope, you can have an expression that utilizes values in the scope, and as the model changes, so does the value of the expression.

Controllers

AngularJS completes the MVC framework through the implementation of controllers. Controllers augment the scope by setting up the initial state or values in the scope and by adding behavior to the scope. For example, you can add a function that sums values in a scope to provide a total such that if the model data behind the scope changes, the total value always changes.

You add controllers to HTML elements by using a directive and then implement them as JavaScript code in the background.

Data Binding

One of the best features of AngularJS is the built-in data binding. Data binding is the process of linking data from the model with what is displayed in a web page. AngularJS provides a very clean interface to link the model data to elements in a web page.

In AngularJS data binding is a two-way process: When data is changed on a web page, the model is updated, and when data is changed in the model, the web page is automatically updated. This way, the model is always the only source for data represented to the user, and the view is just a projection of the model.

Services

Services are the major workhorses in the AngularJS environment. Services are singleton objects that provide functionality for a web app. For example, a common task of web applications is to perform AJAX requests to a web server. AngularJS provides an HTTP service that houses all the functionality to access a web server.

The service functionality is completely independent of context or state, so it can be easily consumed from the components of an application. AngularJS provides a lot of built-in service components for basic uses, such as HTTP requests, logging, parsing, and animation. You can also create your own services and reuse them throughout your code.

Dependency Injection

Dependency injection is a process in which a code component defines dependencies on other components. When the code is initialized, the dependent component is made available for access within the component. AngularJS applications make heavy use of dependency injection.

A common use for dependency injection is consuming services. For example, if you are defining a module that requires access to the web server via HTTP requests, you can inject the HTTP service into the module, and the functionality is available in the module code. In addition, one AngularJS module consumes the functionality of another via dependency.

Compiler

AngularJS provides an HTML complier that will discover directives in the AngularJS template and use the JavaScript directive code to build out extended HTML elements. The AngularJS compiler is loaded into the browser when the AngularJS library is bootstrapped. When loaded, the compiler will search through the HTML DOM in the browser and link in any back-end JavaScript code to the HTML elements, and then the final application view will be rendered to the user.

An Overview of the AngularJS Life Cycle

Now that you understand the components involved in an AngularJS application, you need to understand what happens during the life cycle, which has three phases: bootstrap, compilation, and runtime. Understanding the life cycle of an AngularJS application makes it easier to understand how to design and implement your code.

The three phases of the life cycle of an AngularJS application happen each time a web page is loaded in the browser. The following sections describe these phases of an AngularJS application.

The Bootstrap Phase

The first phase of the AngularJS life cycle is the bootstrap phase, which occurs when the AngularJS JavaScript library is downloaded to the browser. AngularJS initializes its own necessary components and then initializes your module, which the ng-app directive points to. The module is loaded, and any dependencies are injected into your module and made available to code within the module.

The Compilation Phase

The second phase of the AngularJS life cycle is the HTML compilation stage. Initially when a web page is loaded, a static form of the DOM is loaded in the browser. During the compilation phase, the static DOM is replaced with a dynamic DOM that represents the AngularJS view.

This phase involves two parts: traversing the static DOM and collecting all the directives and then linking the directives to the appropriate JavaScript functionality in the AngularJS built-in library or custom directive code. The directives are combined with a scope to produce the dynamic or live view.

The Runtime Data Binding Phase

The final phase of the AngularJS application is the runtime phase, which exists until the user reloads or navigates away from a web page. At that point, any changes in the scope are reflected in the view, and any changes in the view are directly updated in the scope, making the scope the single source of data for the view.

AngularJS behaves differently from traditional methods of binding data. Traditional methods combine a template with data received from the engine and then manipulate the DOM each time the data changes. AngularJS compiles the DOM only once and then links the compiled template as necessary, making it much more efficient than traditional methods.

Separation of Responsibilities

An extremely important part of designing AngularJS applications is the separation of responsibilities. The whole reason you choose a structured framework is to ensure that code is well implemented, easy to follow, maintainable, and testable. Angular provides a very structured framework to work from, but you still need to ensure that you implement AngularJS in the appropriate manner.

The following are a few rules to follow when implementing AngularJS:

- The view acts as the official presentation structure for the application. Indicate any presentation logic as directives in the HTML template of the view.

- If you need to perform any DOM manipulation, do it in a built-in or your own custom directive JavaScript code—and nowhere else.

- Implement any reusable tasks as services and add them to your modules by using dependency injection.

- Ensure that the scope reflects the current state of the model and is the single source for data consumed by the view.

- Ensure that the controller code only acts to augment the scope data and doesn't include any business logic.

- Define controllers within the module namespace and not globally. This ensures that your application can be packaged easily and prevents overwhelming the global namespace.

Integrating AngularJS with Existing JavaScript and jQuery

The fact that AngularJS is based on JavaScript and jQuery makes it tempting to simply try to add it to existing applications to provide data binding or other functionality. That approach will almost always end up in problem code that is difficult to maintain. However, using AngularJS doesn't mean that you need to simply toss out your existing code either. Often you can selectively take working JavaScript/jQuery components and convert them to either directives or services.

This also brings up another issue: when to use the full version of jQuery as opposed to the jQuery lite version that is provided with AngularJS? I know that many people have strong views in both directions. On one hand, you want to keep your implementation as clean and simple as possible. But on the other hand, there might be times when you need functionality that's available only in the full version of jQuery. My take, as always, is to use what makes sense. If I need functionality that is not provided with AngularJS jQuery lite, I will load the full library. I'll discuss the mechanics of loading jQuery as opposed to jQuery lite later in this chapter.

The following steps suggest a method to integrate AngularJS into your existing JavaScript and jQuery applications:

1. Write at least one small AngularJS application from the ground up that uses a model, custom HTML directives, services, and controllers. In other words, in this application, ensure that you have a practical comprehension of the AngularJS separation of responsibilities.

2. Identify the model portion of your code. Specifically, try to separate out the code that augments the model data in the model into controller functions and code that accesses the back-end model data into services.

3. Identify the code that manipulates DOM elements in the view. Try to separate out the DOM manipulation code into well-defined custom directive components and provide an HTML directive for them. Also identify any of the directives for which AngularJS already provides built-in support.

4. Identify other task-based functions and separate them out into services.

5. Isolate the directives and controllers into modules to organize your code.

6. Use dependency injection to link up your services and modules appropriately.

7. Update the HTML templates to use the new directives.

Obviously, in some instances it just doesn't make sense to use much if any of your existing code. However, by running through the preceding steps, you will get well into the design phase of implementing a project using AngularJS and can then make an informed decision.

Adding AngularJS to Your Environment

AngularJS is a client-side JavaScript library, which means the only thing you need to do to implement AngularJS in your environment is to provide a method for the client to get the `angular.js` library file by using a `<script>` tag in the HTML templates.

The simplest method of providing the `angular.js` library is to use the Content Delivery Network (CDN), which provides a URL for downloading the library from a third party. The downside of this method is that you must rely on a third party to serve the library, and if the client cannot connect to that third-party URL, your application will not work. For example, the following `<script>` tag loads the `angular.js` library from Google APIs CDN:

```
<script src="https://ajax.googleapis.com/ajax/libs/angularjs/1.2.5/angular.min.js">
</script>
```

The other method of providing the `angular.js` library is to download it from the AngularJS website (http://angularjs.org) and use your own web server to serve the file to the client. This method takes more effort and also requires extra bandwidth on your web server; however, it might be a better option if you want more control over how the client obtains the library.

Bootstrapping AngularJS in an HTML Document

To implement AngularJS in your web pages, you need to bootstrap the HTML document. Bootstrapping involves two parts. The first part is to define the application module by using the `ng-app` directive, and the second is to load the `angular.js` library in a `<script>` tag.

The `ng-app` directive tells the AngularJS compiler to treat that element as the root of the compilation. The `ng-app` directive is typically loaded in the `<html>` tag to ensure that the entire web page is included; however, you could add it to another container element, and only elements inside that container would be included in the AngularJS compilation and consequently in the AngularJS application functionality.

When possible, you should include the `angular.js` library as one of the last tags, if not the last tag, inside the `<body>` of the HTML. When the `angular.js` script is loaded, the compiler kicks off and begins searching for directives. Loading `angular.js` last allows the web page to load faster.

The following is an example of implementing the `ng-app` and `angular.js` bootstrap in an HTML document:

```
<!doctype html>
<html ng-app="myApp">
  <body>
    <script src="http://code.angularjs.org/1.2.9/angular.min.js"></script>
    <script src="/lib/myApp.js"></script>
  </body>
</html>
```

Using the Global APIs

As you are implementing AngularJS applications, you will find that there are common JavaScript tasks that you need to perform regularly, such as comparing objects, deep copying, iterating through objects, and converting JSON data. AngularJS provides a lot of this basic functionality in the global APIs.

The global APIs are available when the `angular.js` library is loaded, and you can access them by using the `angular` object. For example, to create a deep copy of an object named `myObj`, you use the following syntax:

```
var myCopy = angular.copy(myObj);
```

The following code shows an example of iterating through an array of objects by using the
forEach() global API:

```
var objArr = [{score: 95}, {score: 98}, {score: 92}];
var scores = [];
angular.forEach(objArr, function(value, key){
  this.push(key + '=' + value);
}, scores);
// scores == ['score=95', 'score=98', 'score=92']
```

Table 2.1 lists some of the most useful utilities provided in the global APIs. You will see these
used in a number of examples in this book.

Table 2.1   **Useful Global API Utilities Provided in AngularJS**

Utility	Description
copy(*src*, [*dst*])	Creates a deep copy of the src object or array. If a dst parameter is supplied, it is completely overwritten by a deep copy of the source.
element(*element*)	Returns the DOM element specified as a jQuery element. If you have loaded jQuery before loading AngularJS, the object is a full jQuery object; otherwise, it is only a subset of a jQuery object, using the jQuery lite version built into AngularJS. Table 2.2 lists the jQuery lite methods available in AngularJS.
equals(*o1*, *o2*)	Compares o1 with o2 and returns true if they pass an === comparison.
extend(*dst*, *src*)	Copies all the properties from the src object to the dst object.
forEach(*obj*, *iterator*, [*context*])	Iterates through each object in the obj collection, which can be an object or an array. The iterator specifies a function to call, using the following syntax: function(value, key) The context parameter specifies a JavaScript object that acts as the context, accessible via the this keyword, inside the forEach loop.
fromJson(*json*)	Returns a JavaScript object from a JSON string.
toJson(*obj*)	Returns a JSON string form of the JavaScript object obj.
isArray(*value*)	Returns true if the value parameter passed in is an Array object.
isDate(*value*)	Returns true if the value parameter passed in is a Date object.
isDefined(*value*)	Returns true if the value parameter passed in is a defined object.
isElement(*value*)	Returns true if the value parameter passed in is a DOM element object or a jQuery element object.

Utility	Description
isFunction(*value*)	Returns true if the value parameter passed in is a JavaScript function.
isNumber(*value*)	Returns true if the value parameter passed in is a number.
isObject(*value*)	Returns true if the value parameter passed in is a JavaScript object.
isString(*value*)	Returns true if the value parameter passed in is a String object.
isUndefined(*value*)	Returns true if the value parameter passed in is not defined.
lowercase(*string*)	Returns a lowercase version of the string parameter.
uppercase(*string*)	Returns an uppercase version of the string parameter.

Creating a Basic AngularJS Application

Now that you understand the basic components in the AngularJS framework, the intent and design of the AngularJS framework, and how to bootstrap AngularJS, you are ready to get started implementing AngularJS code. This section walks you through a very basic AngularJS application that implements an HTML template, an AngularJS module, a controller, a scope, and an expression.

For this example it is expected that you have created a basic Node.js web server as described in Chapter 1, "Jumping Into JavaScript." The folder structure for this example will be as follows. Future chapters will have a similar code structure for their examples with just the chapter folder changing:

- **./server.js**: Node.js server that serves up the static content.
- **./images**: Contains any images used in examples in all chapters.
- **./ch01**: Contains any HTML files used for the examples in this chapter.
- **./ch01/js**: Contains the necessary JavaScript for the examples in this chapter.
- **./ch01/css**: Contains the necessary CSS for the examples in this chapter.

After the server.js web server is running, the next step is to implement an AngularJS HTML template, such as first.html in Listing 2.1, and an AngularJS JavaScript module, such as first.js in Listing 2.2.

The following sections describe the important steps in implementing the AngularJS application and the code involved in each step. Each of these steps is described in much more detail in later chapters, so don't get bogged down in them here. What is important at this point is that you understand the process of implementing the template, module, controller, and scope and generally how they interact with each other.

The web page defined by Listings 2.1 and 2.2 is a simple web form in which you type in first and last names and then click a button to display a message, as shown in Figure 2.1.

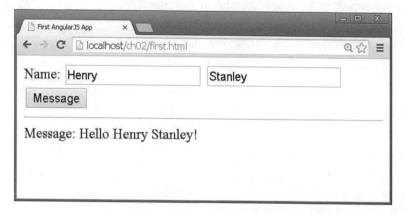

Figure 2.1   Implementing a basic AngularJS web application that uses inputs and a button to manipulate the model and consequently the view.

Loading the AngularJS Library and Your Main Module

Before you can implement an AngularJS application, you need to get the library loaded in an HTML template. The following lines in Listing 2.1 load the angular.js library and then load the first.js JavaScript custom module:

```
15      <script src="http://code.angularjs.org/1.2.9/angular.min.js"></script>
16      <script src="/js/first.js"></script>
```

Defining the AngularJS Application Root Element

The next step is to define the ng-app parameter in the root element so that AngularJS knows where to begin compiling the application. You should also define the module in your JavaScript code to provide a namespace to use when adding controllers, filters, and services.

Line 2 of Listing 2.1 defines the DOM root for an AngularJS module. Notice that ng-app is assigned the module name firstApp, which corresponds to the module in the JavaScript code:

```
02 <html ng-app="firstApp">
```

Line 1 in Listing 2.2 shows the firstApp module object being created in the JavaScript code:

```
01 var firstApp = angular.module('firstApp', []);
```

Adding a Controller to the Template

Next, you need to add a controller for HTML elements that you want the AngularJS module to control. You also need to define the controller in your module code.

Line 7 in Listing 2.1 assigns a controller named `FirstController` to a `<div>` element. This maps the element in the view to a specific controller, which contains a scope:

```
07    <div ng-controller="FirstController">
```

Line 2 in Listing 2.2 shows the `FirstController` code being added to the `firstApp` module:

```
02 firstApp.controller('FirstController', function($scope) {
```

Implementing the Scope Model

After the controller has been defined, you can implement the scope, which involves linking HTML elements to scope variables, initializing the variables in the scope, and providing functionality to handle changes to the scope values.

Lines 9 and 10 in Listing 2.1 are `<input>` elements that are assigned to the `first` and `last` values in the scope. These elements provide a method to update the scope from the browser. If the user types in the input, the scope is also updated:

```
09        <input type="text" ng-model="first">
10        <input type="text" ng-model="last">
```

Lines 3–5 in Listing 2.2 show the initial values of the scope being defined:

```
03    $scope.first = 'Some';
04    $scope.last = 'One';
05    $scope.heading = 'Message: ';
```

Line 11 in Listing 2.1 links a click handler to the `updateMessage()` function defined in the scope:

```
11        <button ng-click='updateMessage()'>Message</button>
```

Lines 6–8 in Listing 2.2 show the `updateMessage()` definition in the scope:

```
06    $scope.updateMessage = function() {
07      $scope.message = 'Hello ' + $scope.first +' '+ $scope.last + '!';
08    };
```

Line 13 implements an expression that displays the value of the `heading` and `message` variables in the scope on the HTML page:

```
13        {{heading + message}}
```

Listing 2.1 `first.html`: A Simple AngularJS Template That Provides Two Input Elements and a Button to Interact with the Model

```
01 <!doctype html>
02 <html ng-app="firstApp">
03   <head>
04     <title>First AngularJS App</title>
05   </head>
06   <body>
07     <div ng-controller="FirstController">
08       <span>Name:</span>
09       <input type="text" ng-model="first">
10       <input type="text" ng-model="last">
11       <button ng-click='updateMessage()'>Message</button>
12       <hr>
13       {{heading + message}}
14     </div>
15     <script src="http://code.angularjs.org/1.2.9/angular.min.js"></script>
16     <script src="js/first.js"></script>
17   </body>
18 </html>
```

Listing 2.2 `first.js`: A Simple AngularJS Module That Implements a Controller to Support the Template in Listing 2.1

```
01 var firstApp = angular.module('firstApp', []);
02 firstApp.controller('FirstController', function($scope) {
03   $scope.first = 'Some';
04   $scope.last = 'One';
05   $scope.heading = 'Message: ';
06   $scope.updateMessage = function() {
07     $scope.message = 'Hello ' + $scope.first +' '+ $scope.last + '!';
08   };
09 });
```

Using jQuery or jQuery Lite in AngularJS Applications

You will be using at least jQuery lite in your AngularJS applications, so it is important to understand the interactions between jQuery, jQuery lite and AngularJS. Even if you are not a jQuery developer, understanding these interactions will help you write better AngularJS applications. If you are a jQuery developer, understanding the interactions will enable you to leverage your jQuery knowledge in your AngularJS applications.

The following sections describe jQuery lite implementation as well as giving a brief introduction to the jQuery/jQuery lite interactions that you will be seeing in your AngularJS applications. The following chapters will expand on this topic as you see some practical examples that utilize jQuery objects in AngularJS applications.

What Is jQuery Lite?

jQuery lite is simply a stripped-down version of jQuery that is built directly into AngularJS. The intent is to provide all the useful features of jQuery and yet keep it constrained within the AngularJS separation of responsibilities paradigm.

Table 2.2 lists the jQuery methods available in jQuery lite along with any restrictions that might apply. The restrictions are necessary to enforce things like manipulating elements only within a custom directive, and so on.

Table 2.2   **jQuery Methods That Are Supported in jQuery Lite**

jQuery Method	Limitations, if any, in jQuery Lite
addClass()	
after()	
append()	
attr()	
bind()	Does not support namespaces, selectors, or eventData.
children()	Does not support selectors.
clone()	
contents()	
css()	
data()	
detach()	
emtyp()	
eq()	
find()	Limited to lookups by tag name.
hasClass()	
html()	
text()	Does not support selectors.
on()	Does not support namespaces, selectors, or eventData.
off()	Does not support namespaces or selectors.
one()	Does not support namespaces or selectors.

jQuery Method	Limitations, if any, in jQuery Lite
parent()	Does not support selectors.
prepend()	
prop()	
ready()	
remove()	
removeAttr()	
removeClass()	
removeData()	
replaceWith()	
toggleClass()	
triggerHandler()	Passes a dummy event object to handlers.
unbind()	Does not support namespaces.
val()	
wrap()	

Table 2.3 lists the additional events and methods that AngularJS adds to jQuery lite objects.

Table 2.3 **Methods and Events Added to jQuery Lite Objects**

Method/Event	Description
$destroy	AngularJS intercepts all jQuery or jQuery lite DOM destruction calls and fires this event on all DOM nodes being removed. This can be used to clean up any third-party bindings to the DOM element before it is removed.
controller(name)	Returns the controller object of the current element or its parent. If no name is specified, the controller associated with the ngController directive is returned. If a name is provided as a directive name, the controller for this directive is returned.
injector()	Returns the injector object of the current element or its parent.
scope()	Returns the scope object of the current element or its parent.
isolateScope()	Returns an isolate scope object if one is attached directly to the current element. This works only on elements that contain a directive that starts a new isolate scope.
inheritedData()	Works the same as the jQuery data() method, but walks up the DOM until a value is found or the top parent element is reached.

Accessing jQuery or jQuery Lite Directly

For most AngularJS applications the jQuery lite library built into AngularJS is sufficient. However, if you need the additional functionality of the full version of jQuery, simply load the jQuery library before loading the AngularJS library. For example:

```
<script src="http://code.jquery.com/jquery-1.11.0.min.js"></script>
<script src="http://code.angularjs.org/1.2.9/angular.min.js"></script>
```

Regardless of whether jQuery lite or the full jQuery library is loaded, jQuery is accessed from the AngularJS code using the `element` attribute of the `angular` variable available when AngularJS is bootstrapped. Essentially, `angular.element` will be an alias for the `jQuery` variable that is normally used in jQuery applications. One of the best ways I've seen this relationship described is as follows:

```
angular.element() === jQuery() === $()
```

Accessing jQuery or jQuery Lite Directly

More often than not, you will be using the jQuery or jQuery lite functionality in jQuery objects that AngularJS creates for you. All element references in AngularJS are always wrapped as jQuery or jQuery lite objects; they are never raw DOM objects.

For example, when you create a directive in AngularJS as discussed later in this book, an element is passed to the link function. That element, as shown here, is a jQuery or jQuery lite object, and you can use the jQuery functionality accordingly:

```
angular.module('myApp', [])
  .directive('myDirective', function() {
      . . .
      link: function(scope, elem, attrs, photosControl) {
        //elem is a jQuery lite object
        elem.addClass(...);
      }
  };
```

Another example of accessing the jQuery functionality is from events that are triggered on AngularJS bindings. For example, consider the following code that uses the `ngClick` binding to bind a browser click event on a `<div>` element to a `clicked()` function in the AngularJS code:

```
<div ng-click="clicked($event)">Click Me</div>
You can access a jQuery version of the object using the following AngularJS code:
$scope.clicked = function(event){
  var jQueryElement = angular.element(event.target);
};
```

Note that it was necessary to use the `angular.element()` method to convert the `target` DOM object into a jQuery object.

Summary

AngularJS is a JavaScript library framework that provides a very structured method for creating websites and web applications. AngularJS structures a web application into a very clean MVC-styled approach. AngularJS scopes provide contextual binding to the data model for the application and are made up of basic JavaScript objects. AngularJS utilizes templates with directives that extend HTML capabilities, enabling you to implement totally customized HTML components.

In this chapter you looked at the different components in an AngularJS application and how they interact with each other. You also learned about the life cycle of an AngularJS application, which involves bootstrap, compilation, and runtime phases. At the end of this chapter, you walked through a step-by-step example of implementing a basic AngularJS application, including a template, module, controller, and scope.

3

Understanding AngularJS Application Dynamics

One of the most important aspects of AngularJS to understand is dependency injection and how it relates to modules. Dependency is a common concept across many server-side languages but has not really been implemented much in JavaScript until AngularJS.

Dependency injection allows AngularJS modules to maintain a very clean, organized form yet more easily access functionality from other modules. When implemented correctly, it also tends to reduce the amount of code by a considerable amount.

This chapter provides a basic overview of dependency injection and then describes how to create modules that provide functionality and how to consume that functionality in other modules as well as other AngularJS components, such as controllers.

Looking at Modules and Dependency Injection

As you begin writing AngularJS applications, it is vital that you understand the basics of modules and dependency injection in the AngularJS world. This seems to be a difficult concept to grasp and implement correctly for some, especially those coming from a more open, anything-goes JavaScript background.

This section introduces you to the concepts behind AngularJS modules and dependency injection. Understanding how modules utilize dependency injection to access functionality in other modules will make it easier for you to implement your code inside the AngularJS framework.

Understanding Modules

AngularJS modules are containers that enable you to compartmentalize and organize your code into concise, clean, reusable chunks. Modules themselves do not provide direct functionality, but they contain instances of other objects that do, such as controllers, filters, services, and animations.

You build a module by defining the objects it provides. Then, by linking together modules through dependency injection, you build a full application.

AngularJS is built on the module principle. Most of the functionality provided by AngularJS is built into a module named ng, which contains most of the directives and services used throughout this book.

Dependency Injection

Dependency injection can be a difficult concept to fully grasp. However, it is a very important part of AngularJS, and after you understand the basics, the AngularJS implementation becomes quite clear. Dependency injection is a well-known design pattern in many server-side languages but has not been used extensively in a JavaScript framework until AngularJS.

The idea of AngularJS dependency injection is to define and dynamically inject a dependency object into another object, making available all the functionality provided by the dependency object. AngularJS provides dependency injection through the use of providers and an injector service.

Providers

A provider is essentially a definition of how to create an instance of an object with all the necessary functionality. Providers should be defined as part of an AngularJS module. A module registers the provider with the injector server. Only one instance of a provider's object is ever created in the AngularJS application.

Injectors

The injector service is responsible for keeping track of instances of provider objects. An injector service instance is created for each module that registers a provider. When a dependency request is made for a provider object, the injector service first checks whether an instance already exists in the injector cache. If so, that instance is used. If no instance is found in the cache, a new instance is created using the provider definition, stored in the cache, and then returned.

Defining an AngularJS Module Object

Creating AngularJS modules is a simple process that involves calling the angular.module() method. This method creates an instance of a Module object, registers it with the injector service, and then returns an instance of the newly created Module object that you can use to implement provider functionality. The angular.module() method uses the following syntax:

```
angular.module(name, [requires], [configFn])
```

The `name` parameter is the name under which the module is registered in the injector service. The `requires` parameter is an array of names of modules that are added to the injector service for this module to use. If you need functionality from another module, you need to add it in the `requires` list. The `ng` module is automatically added to every module instantiated by default, so you have access to the AngularJS providers without explicitly specifying `ng` in the list.

Instances of all dependencies are automatically injected into an instance of a module. Dependencies can be modules, services, and any other objects registered in the injector service. The `configFn` parameter is another function that is called during the module configuration phase. Configuration functions are described in the next section.

The following is an example of creating an AngularJS module with dependencies on the `$window` and `$http` services. The definition also includes a configuration function that adds a value provider named `myValue`:

```
var myModule = angular.module('myModule', ['$window', '$http'], function(){
    $provide.value('myValue', 'Some Value');
});
```

If you do not specify a `requires` parameter, then instead of a `Module` object being created, the already-created instance is returned. For example, the following code overwrites the instance defined previously:

```
var myModule2 = angular.module('myModule', []);
```

However, the following code returns the instance created previously because no dependencies are listed in the `require` array in the parameters list:

```
var myModule3 = angular.module('myModule');
```

Creating Providers in AngularJS Modules

AngularJS provides a number of built-in providers for various objects and services. For example, the `$window` service has a provider that builds the AngularJS service object that enables you to interact with the underlying `Window` object in JavaScript. In addition to these providers, you can create providers of your own to inject functionality into AngularJS application components.

The `Module` object provides several helper methods for adding providers as an alternative to using the `config()` method. These methods are simpler to use and clearer in your code. You can add two types of provider objects to AngularJS modules. Each of these methods accepts two parameters: the name that will be registered with the dependency injector and the provider function that defines how to build the specific object. The following sections describe these methods in more detail.

Specialized AngularJS Object Providers

The `Module` object provides special constructor methods to add providers for the AngularJS objects that you need to implement in your modules. These specialized methods enable you to add definitions for the following types of objects:

- `animation(`*name, animationFactory*`)`
- `controller(`*name, controllerFactory*`)`
- `filter(`*name, filterFactory*`)`
- `directive(`*name, directiveFactory*`)`

The reason these are specialized methods is that there are corresponding `animation`, `controller`, `filter`, and `directive` objects defined in AngularJS for these provider methods.

Each of these objects is covered in more detail in later chapters. For now, here's a quick look at a basic controller definition:

```
var mod = angular.module('myMod', []);
mod.controller('myController', function($scope) {
  $scope.someValue = 'Some Value';
});
```

A simple module named `mod` is created, and then the `controller()` method is called and passed in `myController` along with a `controllerFactory` function. The `controllerFactory` function accepts the `$scope` variable as a parameter. This is because AngularJS has a built-in controller object and knows that all controller objects must receive a scope object as the first parameter.

Service Providers

The service providers are a unique category of providers because there is not already a specific format for the resulting provider objects. Instead, a provider acts as a service to provide functionality. AngularJS provides some specific creation methods for building services and exposes them through the following methods:

- **`value`***(name, object)*: This is the most basic of all providers. The `object` parameter is simply assigned to `name`, so there is a direct correlation in the injector between the `name` value and the `object` value.
- **`constant`***(name, object)*: This is similar to the `value()` method, but the value is not changeable. Also, `constant()` methods are applied before other provider methods.
- **`factory`***(name, factoryFunction)*: This method uses the `factoryFunction` parameter to build an object that will be provided by the injector.
- **`service`***(name, serviceFactory)*: This method adds the concept of implementing a more object-oriented approach to the provider object. Much of the built-in functionality of AngularJS is provided through service providers.

- **provider** *(name, providerFactory)*: This method is the core for all the other methods. Although it provides the most functionality, it is not used frequently because the other methods are simpler.

Later chapters cover these objects in more detail. For now, here's a quick example of some basic value and `constant` definitions:

```
var mod = angular.module('myMod', []);
mod.constant("cID", "ABC");
mod.value('counter', 0);
mod.value('image', {name:'box.jpg', height:12, width:20});
```

A simple module named `mod` is created, and then the `constant()` and two `value()` providers are defined. The values defined in these methods are registered in the injector server for the `myMod` module and are then accessible by name.

Implementing Providers and Dependency Injection

After you have defined a module and appropriate providers, you can add the module as a dependency to other modules, controllers, and various other AngularJS objects. You can set the value of the `$inject` property of the object that depends on the providers. The `$inject` property contains an array of provider names that should be injected into it.

For example, the following code defines a basic controller that accepts the `$scope` and `appMsg` parameters. Then the `$inject` property is set to an array that contains `$scope`, which is the AngularJS scope service that provides access to the scope and a custom `appMsg`. Both `$scope` and `appMsg` are injected into the `myController` function:

```
var myController = function($scope, appMsg) {
  $scope.message = appMsg;
};
controller['$inject'] = ['$scope', 'appMsg'];
myApp.myController('controllerA', controller);
```

This method can become a bit clumsy when you're implementing certain objects, so AngularJS also provides a bit more elegant method for injecting the dependencies, using the following syntax in place of the normal constructor function:

```
[providerA, providerB, . . ., function(objectA, objectB, . . .) {} ]
```

For example, the preceding code can also be written this way:

```
myApp.controller('controllerA', ['$scope', 'appMsg', function($scope, appMsg) {
  $scope.message = appMsg;
}]);
```

It is critical that you understand dependency injection before continuing, so let's take a look at a couple of examples. The following sections provide sample listings that implement dependency injection in AngularJS applications.

Injecting a Built-in Provider into a Controller

Listing 3.1 shows a very basic example of using dependency injection to inject functionality from the $scope and $window service into an AngularJS controller. The AngularJS app defined in Listing 3.1 is very simple. On line 2 it defines a basic controller and uses dependency injection to inject the $scope and $window service, and then in lines 3 and 4 it uses the $window service to display an alert pop-up with a message stored in the $scope.

Listing 3.2 shows the HTML page that uses the myApp module defined in Listing 3.1 and implements the view for controllerA. Figure 3.1 shows the resulting web page and alert message.

Listing 3.1   `inject_builtin.js`: Implementing Dependency Injection of Built-in Services in a Controller

```
01 var myMod = angular.module('myApp', []);
02 myMod.controller('controllerA', ['$scope', '$window',
03                                  function($scope, $window) {
04    $scope.message = "My Module Has Loaded!";
05    $window.alert($scope.message);
06 }]);
```

Listing 3.2   `inject_builtin.html`: Using HTML Code to Implement an AngularJS Module That Implements Dependency Injection

```
01 <!doctype html>
02 <html ng-app="myApp">
03   <head>
04     <title>AngularJS Dependency Injection</title>
05   </head>
06   <body>
07     <div ng-controller="controllerA">
08       <h2>This Page has an Alert</h2>
09     </div><hr>
10     <script src="http://code.angularjs.org/1.2.9/angular.min.js"></script>
11     <script src="js/inject_builtin.js"></script>
12   </body>
13 </html>
```

Figure 3.1   Implementing dependency injection of the $window service to display an alert message from the $scope.

Implementing a Custom Provider and Injecting It into a Controller

Listing 3.3 shows how to implement dependency injection with two modules, each with a value provider and a controller. Lines 2 and 8 add the value providers. Lines 3 and 9 use dependency injection to inject the value providers into the controllers for each module.

Notice in line 6 that the definition for the myApp module includes the myMod module in its dependency list. This injects myMod, including the controllerB functionality, enclosed inside.

Listing 3.4 shows HTML that implements the myApp module as the AngularJS application. Notice that it uses both the controllerA and the controllerB controllers. They can be used because the myMod module was injected into the myApp module. Figure 3.2 shows the resulting web page, with a different message from each module's controller.

Listing 3.3 `inject_custom.js`: Implementing Dependency Injection in Controller and Module Definitions

```
01 var myMod = angular.module('myMod', []);
02 myMod.value('modMsg', 'Hello from My Module');
03 myMod.controller('controllerB', ['$scope', 'modMsg',
04                                 function($scope, msg) {
05   $scope.message = msg;
06 }]);
07 var myApp = angular.module('myApp', ['myMod']);
08 myApp.value('appMsg', 'Hello from My App');
09 myApp.controller('controllerA', ['$scope', 'appMsg',
10                                 function($scope, msg) {
11   $scope.message = msg;
12 }]);
```

Listing 3.4 `inject_custom.html`: Using HTML Code to Implement an AngularJS Module That Depends on Another Module

```
01 <!doctype html>
02 <html ng-app="myApp">
03   <head>
04     <title>AngularJS Dependency Injection</title>
05   </head>
06   <body>
07     <div ng-controller="controllerA">
08       <h2>Application Message:</h2>
09       {{message}}
10     </div><hr>
11     <div ng-controller="controllerB">
12       <h2>Module Message:</h2>
13       {{message}}
14     </div>
15     <script src="http://code.angularjs.org/1.2.9/angular.min.js"></script>
16     <script src="/js/injector_custom.js"></script>
17   </body>
18 </html>
```

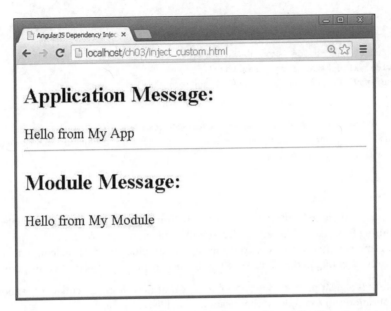

Figure 3.2   Implementing dependency injection to provide additional functionality to modules and controllers.

Applying Configuration and Run Blocks to Modules

Now that you understand the relationship between modules and dependency injection, you need to look at the process of implementing AngularJS modules. AngularJS modules are implemented in two phases: the configuration phase and the run phase. The following sections discuss these phases and the basic process of adding providers to an AngularJS module.

Adding Configuration Blocks

The AngularJS module configuration phase is executed when a module is being defined. During this phase, any providers are registered with the dependency injector. You should put only configuration and provider code inside the configuration block.

You implement the configuration block by calling the `config()` method on the instance of the `Module` object, using the following syntax:

```
config(function([injectable, . . .]))
```

A function with the `injectable` parameters is passed in. The `injectable` parameters are typically provider services functions such as `$provide`.

The following is an example of a basic configuration block:

```
var myModule = angular.module('myModule', []).
  config(function($provide, $filterProvider) {
    $provide.value("startTime", new Date());
    $filterProvider.register('myFilter', function(){});
});
```

Notice that the $provide and $filterProvider services are passed into the config function. They are used to register a value provider named startTime and a filer provider named myFilter with the injector service.

Adding Run Blocks

After an entire configuration block has finished, the run phase of an AngularJS module can execute. During this phase, you can implement any code necessary to instantiate the module. You cannot implement any provider code during the run block because the entire module should already be configured and registered with the dependency injector by this point.

The run block is a great place to put event handlers that need to be executed at the root level for the application (for example, authentication handlers).

You implement the run block by calling the run() method of the Module object, using the following syntax:

```
run(function([injectable, . . .]))
```

A function with the instance injectable parameters is passed in. The injectable parameters should only be instances of injectors because configuration should already have been completed.

The following is a basic implementation of the run block continued from the example:

```
myModule.run(function(startTime) {
  startTime.setTime((new Date()).getTime());
});
```

Notice that the startTime instance defined in the config() section shown previously is passed into the run() function. This allows the run() function to update the startTime provider to a new value.

Implementing Configuration and Run Blocks

Listing 3.5 shows an example of implementing very basic configuration and run blocks. In lines 2–8, the config() method is used to implement two providers, configTime and runTime, that are JavaScript Date objects. Notice that in lines 5–7 a simple loop is implemented to inject a delay simulating a delay that might be caused during configuration.

In lines 9–11 the run() method is implemented. Notice that it accepts the configTime and runTime instances that were created during configuration and updates the runTime value to the current time. Then in Lines 12–16 a controller is implemented that sets the configTime and runTime values in the scope.

Listing 3.6 shows HTML that implements the myApp module and displays the configTime and runTime values. You can see that the injected delay results in different times for the values. Figure 3.3 shows the resulting web page.

Listing 3.5   `config_run_blocks.js`: Implementing Configuration and Run Blocks in an AngularJS Module

```
01 var myModule = angular.module('myApp', []);
02 myModule.config(function($provide) {
03     $provide.value("configTime", new Date());
04     $provide.value("runTime", new Date());
05     for(var x=0; x<1000000000; x++){
06       var y = Math.sqrt(Math.log(x));
07     }
08 });
09 myModule.run(function(configTime, runTime) {
10   runTime.setTime((new Date()).getTime());
11 });
12 myModule.controller('controllerA',['$scope', 'configTime', 'runTime',
13     function($scope, configTime, runTime){
14   $scope.configTime = configTime;
15   $scope.runTime = runTime;
16 }]);
```

Listing 3.6   `config_run_blocks.html`: Using HTML Code to Display the configTime and runTime Values Generated in the Configuration and Run Blocks of the AngularJS Module

```
01 <!doctype html>
02 <html ng-app="myApp">
03   <head>
04     <title>AngularJS Configuration and Run Blocks</title>
05   </head>
06   <body>
07     <div ng-controller="controllerA">
08       <hr>
09       <h2>Config Time:</h2>
10       {{configTime}}
11       <hr>
12       <h2>Run Time:</h2>
13       {{runTime}}
14     </div><hr>
```

```
15      <script src="http://code.angularjs.org/1.2.9/angular.min.js"></script>
16      <script src="js/config_run_blocks.js"></script>
17   </body>
18 </html>
```

Figure 3.3   Implementing configuration and run blocks that set and utilize JavaScript Date objects to display the time executed for each.

Summary

Dependency injection enables you to define provider functionality that can be injected into other AngularJS components. The provider functionality is contained inside modules and registered with an injector service. Providers define how to build the functionality so that when another component defines a dependency on a provider, an instance of the provider object can be created and injected.

AngularJS provides a fairly robust dependency injection model that enables you to define different types of service providers. Using dependency injection rather than global definitions makes your code more modularized and easier to maintain. In this chapter you were introduced to the dependency injection model and have seen how to implement it in both modules and a controller component.

4

Implementing the Scope as a Data Model

One of the most important aspects of an AngularJS application is scope. Scope not only provides the data represented in a model but also binds together all the other components of the AngularJS application, such as modules, controllers, services, and templates. This chapter explains the relationships between scope and other AngularJS components.

Scope provides the binding mechanism that enables DOM elements and other code to be updated when changes occur in the model data. In this chapter you will learn about the root scope and child scopes. You will also learn about the scope hierarchies and how to implement them.

Understanding Scopes

In AngularJS, the scope acts as a data model for an application. It is one of the most critical parts of any application that relies on data in any fashion because it acts as the glue that binds together the views, business logic, and server-side data. Understanding how scopes work enables you to design your AngularJS applications to be more efficient, use less code, and be easier to follow.

The following sections discuss the relationships between scope and applications, controllers, templates, and server-side data. There is also a section that covers the life cycle of scope, to help you see how scope is built, manipulated, and updated during the application life cycle.

The Relationship Between the Root Scope and Applications

When an application is bootstrapped, a root scope is created. The root scope stores data at the application level, and you can access it by using the `$rootScope` service. The root scope data should be initialized in the `run()` block of the module, but you can also access it in components of the module. To illustrate this point, the following code defines a value at the root scope level and then accesses it in a controller:

```
angular.module('myApp', [])
.run(function($rootScope) {
    $rootScope.rootValue = 5;
})
.controller('myController', function($scope, $rootScope) {
  $scope.value = 10;
  $scope.difference = function() {
        return $rootScope.rootValue - $scope.value;
    };
});
```

The Relationship Between Scopes and Controllers

Controllers are pieces of code that are intended to provide business logic by augmenting scope. You create controllers by using the `controller()` method on the `Model` object of an application. This function registers a controller as a provider in the module, but it does not create an instance of the controller. That occurs when the `ng-controller` directive is linked in an AngularJS template.

The `controller()` method accepts the controller name as the first parameter and an array of dependencies as the second parameter. For example, the following code defines a controller that uses dependency injection to access a `value` provider named `start`:

```
angular.module('myApp', []).
  value('start', 200).
  controller('Counter', ['$scope', 'start',
                          function($scope, startingValue) {
  }]);
```

When a new instance of a controller is created in AngularJS, a new child scope specific to that controller is also created and is accessible via the `$scope` service that is injected into the preceding `Counter` controller. Also in the example shown previously, the `start` provider is injected into the controller and passed to the controller function as `startingValue`. The parameter injection is based on their position in the array passed to the `controller()` function.

The controller must initialize the state of a scope that is created and added to it. The controller is also responsible for any business logic attached to that scope. This can mean handling update changes to the scope, manipulating scope values, or emitting events based on the state of the scope.

Listing 4.1 shows how to implement a controller that utilizes dependency injection, initializes some values, and implements rudimentary business logic, using `inc()`, `dec()`, and `calcDiff()` functions. Notice in lines 5–8 that several values are stored in the scope variables `start`, `current`, `difference`, and `change`. Those values are subsequently manipulated in the `inc()`, `dec()`, and `calcDiff()` functions.

Listing 4.2 shows a basic AngularJS HTML template that provides the view to see and manipulate the values stored in the scope. Figure 4.1 shows the web page in action. You can set the increment/decrement value and then click on +/- buttons to decrement the current value and see the difference change in the scope.

Listing 4.1 `scope_controller.js`: Implementing a Basic Controller That Uses Dependency Injection, Initializes Scope Values, and Implements Business Logic

```
01 angular.module('myApp', []).
02   value('start', 200).
03   controller('Counter', ['$scope', 'start',
04                          function($scope, start) {
05     $scope.start = start;
06     $scope.current = start;
07     $scope.difference = 0;
08     $scope.change = 1;
09     $scope.inc = function() {
10       $scope.current += $scope.change;
11       $scope.calcDiff();
12     };
13     $scope.dec = function() {
14       $scope.current -= $scope.change;
15       $scope.calcDiff();
16     };
17     $scope.calcDiff = function() {
18       $scope.difference = $scope.current - $scope.start;
19     };
20   }]);
```

Listing 4.2 `scope_controller.html`: HTML Template That Enables You to See the Data in the Scope Change Dynamically Based on Incrementing and Decrementing Values

```
01 <!doctype html>
02 <html ng-app="myApp">
03   <head>
04     <title>AngularJS Basic Scope</title>
05   </head>
06   <body>
07     <div ng-controller="Counter">
08       <span>Change Amount:</span>
09       <input type="number" ng-model="change"><hr>
10       <span>Starting Value:</span>
11       {{start}}
12       <br>
13       <span>CurrentValue:</span>
14       {{current}}
```

```
15        <button ng-click='inc()'>+</button>
16        <button ng-click='dec()'>-</button><hr>
17        <span>Difference:</span>
18        {{difference}}
19      </div>
20      <script src="http://code.angularjs.org/1.3.0/angular.min.js"></script>
21      <script src="js/scope_controller.js"></script>
22    </body>
23 </html>
```

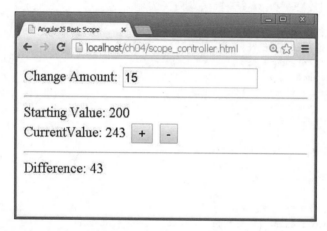

Figure 4.1   A basic AngularJS application that stores initial and current values in the scope and then displays the difference to illustrate scope data interaction.

The Relationship Between Scopes and Templates

Templates provide the view for an AngularJS application. HTML elements are defined as controllers, using the `ng-controller` attribute. Inside a controller HTML element and its children, the scope for that controller is available for expressions and other AngularJS functionality.

Values in a scope can be directly linked to the values of `<input>`, `<select>`, and `<textarea>` elements in the template, using the `ng-model` directive. This directive links the value of an element to a property name in the scope. When the user changes the value of the input element, the scope is automatically updated. For example, the following links the value of a number of an `<input>` element to the scope named `valueA`:

```
<input type="number" ng-model="valueA" />
```

You can add scope properties and even functions to expressions in a template by using the {{expression}} syntax. The code inside the brackets is evaluated, and the results are displayed in the rendered view. For example, if a scope contains properties named valueA and valueB, you can reference these properties in an expression in the template as shown here:

{{valueA + valueB}}

You can also use scope properties and functions when defining AngularJS directives in a template. For example, the ng-click directive binds the browser click event to a function in a scope named addValues() and passes the values of properties valueA and valueB in the scope:

<span ng-click="addValues(valueA, valueB")>Add Values{{valueA}} & {{valueB}}</span>

Notice that in this code, the {{}} brackets are required. However, in the addValues() function call they are not required. That is because ng-click and other AngularJS directives automatically evaluate as expressions.

The code in Listings 4.3 and 4.4 puts all these concepts together in a very basic example to make it easy to understand the relationship between the model and the scope. Listing 4.2 implements a controller named SimpleTemplate that initializes a scope with three values: valueA, valueB, and valueC. The scope also contains a function named addValues() that accepts two parameters and adds them together to set the value of $scope.valueC.

Listing 4.4 implements a template that initializes the SimpleTemplate controller defined in Listing 4.3. Lines 8 and 9 link the scope properties valueA and valueB to <input> elements by using ng-model. Line 10 uses the values of valueA and valueB in the scope to display the expression. Line 11 adds valueA and valueB in the scope to display the added value.

Lines 12 and 13 implement an <input> element that uses ng-click to bind the browser click event to the addValues() function in the scope. Notice that valueA and valueB are passed in as parameters to the function.

Figure 4.2 shows this simple application in a web browser. As the two input elements are changed, the expressions change automatically. However, the valueC expression changes only when the Click to Add Values element is clicked.

Listing 4.3 **scope_template.js: Implementing a Basic Controller to Support Template Functionality**

```
01 angular.module('myApp', []).
02   controller('SimpleTemplate', function($scope) {
03     $scope.valueA = 5;
04     $scope.valueB = 7;
05     $scope.valueC = 12;
06     $scope.addValues = function(v1, v2) {
07       var v = angular.$rootScope;
08       $scope.valueC = v1 + v2;
09     };
10   });
```

Listing 4.4 **scope_template.html: HTML Template Code That Implements a Controller and Various HTML Fields Linked to the Scope**

```
01 <!doctype html>
02 <html ng-app="myApp">
03   <head>
04     <title>AngularJS Scope and Templates</title>
05   </head>
06   <body>
07     <div ng-controller="SimpleTemplate">
08       ValueA: <input type="number" ng-model="valueA" /><br>
09       ValueB: <input type="number" ng-model="valueB" /><br><br>
10       Expression: {{valueA}} + {{valueB}}<br><br>
11       Live Expression Value: {{valueA + valueB}}<br><br>
12       <input type="button" ng-click="addValues(valueA, valueB)"
13         value ="Click to Add Values {{valueA}} & {{valueB}}" /><br>
14       Clicked Expression Value: {{valueC}}<br>
15     </div>
16     <script src="http://code.angularjs.org/1.3.0/angular.min.js"></script>
17     <script src="js/scope_template.js"></script>
18   </body>
19 </html>
```

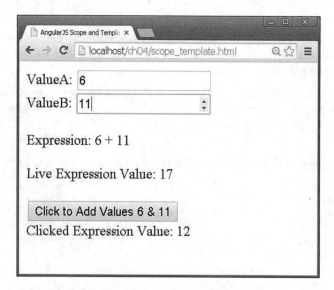

Figure 4.2 A basic AngularJS template that implements a controller and links several fields to the scope to provide both input of values and displayed results.

The Relationship Between Scope and Back-End Server Data

Often data that is used for an AngularJS application comes from a back-end data source such as a database. In such instances, the scope still acts as the definitive source of data for the AngularJS application. You should use the following rules when interacting with data that is coming from the server side:

- Access data from the database or other back-end sources via AngularJS services, which are discussed in Chapter 9, "Implementing AngularJS Services in Web Applications." This includes both reading and updating data.

- Ensure that data read from the server updates the scope, which in turn updates the view. Avoid the temptation to manipulate the HTML values directly from the database, which can lead to the scope becoming out of sync with the view.

- Reflect changes that are made to the database or other back-end source in scope as well. You can do this by first updating the scope and then updating the database using a service, or you can update the database and then use the results from the database to repopulate the appropriate values in the scope.

The Scope Life Cycle

Scope data goes through a life cycle while the application is loaded in the browser. Understanding this life cycle will help you understand the interaction between scope and other AngularJS components, especially templates.

Scope data goes through the following life cycle phases:

1. Creation

2. Watcher registration

3. Model mutation

4. Mutation observation

5. Scope destruction

These life cycle phases are described in the sections that follow.

The Creation Phase

The creation phase occurs when a scope is initialized. Bootstrapping the application creates a root scope. Linking the template creates child scopes when `ng-controller` or `ng-repeat` directives are encountered.

Also during the creation phase, a digest loop is created that interacts with the browser event loop. The digest loop is responsible for updating DOM elements with changes made to the model, as well as executing any registered watcher functions. Although you should never need to execute a digest loop manually, you can do so by executing the `$digest()` method on the scope. For example, the following evaluates any asynchronous changes and then executes the watch functions on the scope:

```
$scope.$digest()
```

The Watcher Registration Phase

The watcher registration phase registers watches for values in the scope that are represented in the template. These watches propagate model changes automatically to the DOM elements.

You can also register your own watch functions on a scope value by using the `$watch()` method. This method accepts a scope property name as the first parameter and then a callback function as the second parameter. The old and new values are passed to the callback function when the property is changed in the scope.

For example, the following adds a watch to the property `watchedItem` in the scope and increments a counter each time it is changed:

```
$scope.watchedItem = 'myItem';
$scope.counter = 0;
$scope.$watch('name', function(newValue, oldValue) {
  $scope.watchedItem = $scope.counter + 1;
});
```

The Model Mutation Phase

The model mutation phase occurs when data in the scope changes. When you make changes in your AngularJS code, a scope function called `$apply()` updates the model and calls the `$digest()` function to update the DOM and watches. This is how changes made in your AngularJS controllers or by the `$http`, `$timeout`, and `$interval` services are automatically updated in the DOM.

You should always try to make changes to scope inside the AngularJS controller or those services. However, if you must make changes to the scope outside the AngularJS realm, you need to call `scope.$apply()` on the scope to force the model and DOM to be updated correctly. The `$apply()` method accepts an expression as the only parameter. The expression is evaluated and returned, and the `$digest()` method is called to update the DOM and watches.

The Mutation Observation Phase

The mutation observation phase occurs when the `$digest()` method is executed by the digest loop, an `$apply()` call, or manually. When `$digest()` executes, it evaluates all watches for changes. If a value has changed, `$digest()` calls the `$watch` listener and updates the DOM.

The Scope Destruction Phase

The `$destroy()` method removes scopes from the browser memory. The AngularJS libraries automatically call this method when child scopes are no longer needed. The `$destroy()` method stops `$digest()` calls and removes watches, allowing the memory to be reclaimed by the browser garbage collector.

Implementing Scope Hierarchy

A great feature of scopes is that they are organized in a hierarchy. The hierarchy helps you keep scopes organized and relevant to the context of the view they represent. There is a root scope at the AngularJS module level and then child scopes can be implemented in sub-components such as controllers or directives. Child scopes can be nested within each other creating a hierarchy structure.

> **Note**
>
> The $digest() method uses the scope hierarchy to propagate scope changes to the appropriate watchers and the DOM elements.

Scope hierarchies are created automatically based on the location of ng-controller statements in the AngularJS template. For example, the following template code defines two <div> elements that create instances of controllers that are siblings:

```
<div ng-controller="controllerA"> . . . </div>
<div ng-controller="controllerB"> . . . </div>
```

However, the following template code defines controllers in which controllerA is the parent of controllerB:

```
<div ng-controller="controllerA">
  <div ng-controller="controllerB"> . . . </div>
</div>
```

The scope hierarchy works similar to the way object inheritance works in OO languages. You can access the values of parent scopes from a controller, but you can't access the values of sibling or children scopes. If you add a property name in a child scope, it does not overwrite the parent but creates a property of the same name in the child scope that has a different value from the parent.

Listings 4.5 and 4.6 implement a basic scope hierarchy to demonstrate how scopes work in a hierarchy. Listing 4.5 creates an application with three controllers, each with two scope items defined. They all share the common scope property title and the scope properties valueA, valueB, and valueC.

Listing 4.6 creates the three controllers in an AngularJS template. Figure 4.3 shows the rendered AngularJS application. Notice that the value of the title property in all three scopes is different. That is because a new title property is created for each level in the hierarchy.

Lines 17–19 display the valueA, valueB, and valueC properties. These values are read from three different levels in the scope hierarchy. The application shows that as you increment the value in the parent scope, a DOM element in a child controller is updated with the new value.

Listing 4.5 `scope_hierarchy.js`: Implementing a Basic Scope Hierarchy with Access to Properties at Each Level

```
01 angular.module('myApp', []).
02   controller('LevelA', function($scope) {
03     $scope.title = "Level A"
04     $scope.valueA = 1;
05     $scope.inc = function() {
06       $scope.valueA++;
07     };
08   }).
09   controller('LevelB', function($scope) {
10     $scope.title = "Level B"
11     $scope.valueB = 1;
12     $scope.inc = function() {
13       $scope.valueB++;
14     };
15   }).
16   controller('LevelC', function($scope) {
17     $scope.title = "Level C"
18     $scope.valueC = 1;
19     $scope.inc = function() {
20       $scope.valueC++;
21     };
22   });
```

Listing 4.6 `scope_hierarchy.html`: HTML Template Code That Implements a Hierarchy of Controllers and Renders Results from the Multiple Levels of Scope

```
01 <!doctype html>
02 <html ng-app="myApp">
03 <head>
04 <title>AngularJS Scope Hierarchy</title>
05 </head>
06 <body>
07   <div ng-controller="LevelA">
08     <h3>{{title}}</h3>
09     ValueA = {{valueA}} <input type="button" ng-click="inc()" value="+" />
10     <div ng-controller="LevelB"><hr>
11       <h3>{{title}}</h3>
12       ValueA = {{valueA}}<br>
13       ValueB = {{valueB}}
14       <input type="button" ng-click="inc()" value="+" />
15       <div ng-controller="LevelC"><hr>
16         <h3>{{title}}</h3>
17         ValueA = {{valueA}}<br>
18         ValueB = {{valueB}}<br>
```

```
19          ValueC = {{valueC}}
20            <input type="button" ng-click="inc()" value="+" />
21        </div>
22      </div>
23    </div>
24    <script src="http://code.angularjs.org/1.3.0/angular.min.js"></script>
25    <script src="js/scope_hierarchy.js"></script>
26  </body>
27  </html>
```

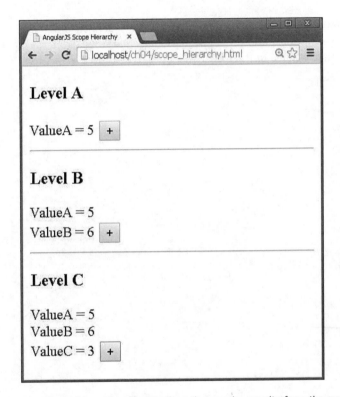

Figure 4.3   Implementing a hierarchy of controllers that render results from the multiple levels of scope.

Summary

A scope is the definitive source for data in AngularJS applications. A scope has direct relationships with the template views, controllers, modules, and services and acts as the glue that binds the application together. A scope also acts as a representation of a database or another server-side data source.

The scope life cycle is linked to the browser event loop so that changes in the browser can change the scope, and changes in the scope are reflected in the DOM elements that are bound to the scope. You can also add custom watch functions that are notified when the scope changes.

Scopes are organized into hierarchies, and the root scope is defined at that application level. Each instance of a controller also gets an instance of a child scope. From the child scopes you can access data that is stored in the parent scope hierarchy.

Using AngularJS Templates to Create Views

AngularJS templates provide a framework to represent the application view to the user. AngularJS templates contain expressions, filters, and directives that define additional functionality and behavior to the DOM elements. The templates are built on top of normal HTML and simply extend the functionality of HTML by adding additional elements and attributes.

This chapter focuses on AngularJS templates, as well as expressions and filters. Expressions enable you to implement JavaScript-like code alongside the HTML code in a template. Filters enable you to modify data values before you display them—for example, to format text.

Understanding Templates

AngularJS templates are fairly straightforward yet very powerful and easy to extend. Templates are based on standard HTML documents but extend the HTML functionality with three additional components:

- **Expressions:** Expressions are bits of JavaScript-like code that are evaluated within the context of a scope. Expressions are denoted by {{}} brackets. The results of an expression are added to a compiled HTML web page. Expressions can be placed in normal HTML text or in the values of attributes, as shown here:

  ```
  <p>{{1+2}}</p>
  href="/myPage.html/{{hash}}"
  ```

- **Filters:** Filters transform the appearance of data that is placed on a web page. For example, a filter can convert a number from the scope into a currency string or a time string.

- **Directives:** Directives are new HTML element names or attribute names within HTML elements. They add to and modify the behavior of HTML elements to provide data binding, event handling, and other support to an AngularJS application.

The following code snippet shows an example of implementing directives, expressions, and filters. The `ng-model="msg"` attribute is a directive that binds the value of the `<input>` element to `msg` in the scope. The code in the `{{}}` brackets is an expression that applies the uppercase filter:

```
<div>
  <input ng-model="msg">
  {{msg | uppercase}}
</div>
```

When you load an AngularJS web page into a browser, you load it in a raw state, containing template code along with HTML code. The initial DOM is built from that web page. When the AngularJS application is bootstrapped, the AngularJS template compiles into the DOM, dynamically adjusting the values, event bindings, and other properties of the DOM elements to the directives, expressions, and filters in the template.

During compilation, HTML tags and attributes are normalized to support the fact that AngularJS is case-sensitive, whereas HTML is not. Normalization does two things:

- Strips the `x-` and `data-` prefixes from the front of elements and attributes.

- Convert names with : or - or _ to camelCase.

For example, all of the following normalize to `ngModel`:

```
ng-model
data-ng-model
x-ng:model
ng_model
```

Using Expressions

Using expressions is the simplest way to represent data from the scope in an AngularJS view. Expressions are encapsulated blocks of code inside brackets: `{{expression}}`. The AngularJS compiler compiles an expression into HTML elements so that the results of the expression are displayed. For example, look at the following expressions:

```
{{1+5}}
{{'One' + 'Two'}}
```

Based on those expressions, the web page displays these values:

```
6
OneTwo
```

Expressions are bound to the data model, which provides two huge benefits. First, you can use the property names and functions that are defined in the scope inside your expressions. Second, because the expressions are bound to the scope, when data in the scope changes, so do the expressions. For example, say that the scope contains the following values:

```
$scope.name='Brad';
$scope.score=95;
```

You can directly reference the name and score values in the template expressions as shown here:

```
Name: {{name}}
Score: {{score}}
Adjusted: {{score+5}}
```

AngularJS expressions are similar to JavaScript expressions in several ways, but they differ in these ways:

- **Attribute evaluation:** Property names are evaluated against the scope model instead of against the global JavaScript namespace.

- **More forgiving:** Expressions do not throw exceptions when they encounter undefined or null variable types; instead, they treat these as having no value.

- **No flow control:** Expressions do not allow JavaScript conditionals or loops. Also, you cannot throw an error inside an expression.

AngularJS evaluates the strings used to define the value of directives as expressions. This enables you to include expression-type syntax within a definition. For example, when you set the value of the ng-click directive in the template, you specify an expression. Inside that expression, you can reference scope variable and use other expression syntax, as shown here:

```
<span ng-click="scopeFunction()"></span>
<span ng-click="scopeFunction(scopeVariable, 'stringParameter')"></span>
<span ng-click="scopeFunction(5*scopeVariable)"></span>
```

Since the AngularJS template expressions have access to the scope, you can also make changes to the scope inside the AngularJS expression. For example, the following ng-click directive changes the value of msg inside the scope model:

```
<span ng-click="msg='clicked'"></span>
```

The following sections take you through some examples of utilizing the expression capability in AngularJS.

Using Basic Expressions

In this exercise you get a chance to see how AngularJS expressions handle rendering of strings and numbers. The purpose of this exercise is to illustrate how AngularJS evaluates expressions that contain strings and numbers as well as basic mathematical operators.

The code in Listing 5.1 is just a simple AngularJS application with a controller named myController. The controller is empty because none of the expressions accesses the scope.

The code in Listing 5.2 is an AngularJS template that contains several types of expressions wrapped in {{ }} brackets. Some of the expressions are just numbers or strings, some include the + operation to combine strings and/or numbers, and one applies a === operator to compare two numbers.

Figure 5.1 shows the rendered web page. Note that numbers and strings are rendered directly to the final view. Adding strings and numbers together enables you to build text strings that are rendered to the view. Also note that using a comparison operator renders the word true or false to the view.

Listing 5.1   **expressions_basic.js: Basic AngularJS Application Code with Empty Controller**

```
01 angular.module('myApp', [])
02   .controller('myController', function($scope) {
03   });
```

Listing 5.2   **expressions_basic.html: Applying Basic Strings and Numbers with Simple Math Operations to an AngularJS Template**

```
01 <!doctype html>
02 <html ng-app="myApp">
03   <head>
04     <title>AngularJS Expressions</title>
05     <style>
06       p{margin:0px;}
07       p:after{color:red;}
08     </style>
09   </head>
10   <body>
11     <div ng-controller="myController">
12       <h1>Expressions</h1>
13       Number:<br>
14       {{5}}<hr>
15       String:<br>
16       {{'My String'}}<hr>
17       Adding two strings together:<br>
18       {{'String1' + ' ' + 'String2'}}<hr>
19       Adding two numbers together:<br>
20       {{5+5}}<hr>
21       Adding strings and numbers together:<br>
22       {{5 + '+' + 5 + '='}}{{5+5}}<hr>
23       Comparing two numbers with each other:<br>
24       {{5===5}}<hr>
25     <script src="http://code.angularjs.org/1.3.0/angular.min.js"></script>
26     <script src="js/expressions_basic.js"></script>
27   </body>
28 </html>
```

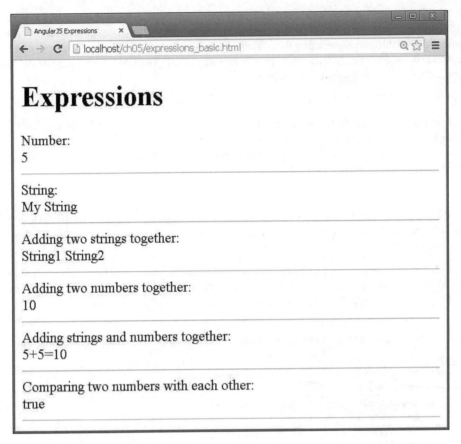

Figure 5.1   Using AngularJS expressions that contain strings, numbers, and basic math operations.

Interacting with the Scope in Expressions

Now that you have seen some basic AngularJS expressions, let's take a look at how to interact with the scope inside AngularJS expressions. In the previous example all the input for the expressions came from explicit strings or numbers. This example illustrates the true power of AngularJS expressions that come from interacting with the model.

The code in Listing 5.3 implements a basic AngularJS application with a controller. The controller contains the variables speed, vehicle, newSpeed, and newVehicle in the scope. It also includes three functions, upper, lower, and setValues. These variables and functions are utilized in AngularJS expressions in the template shown in Listing 5.4.

The code in Listing 5.4 implements an AngularJS template that applies AngularJS expressions that use values from the scope to render text to the screen as well as act as parameters to functions. The first thing to note is that the variable names in the scope can be used directly in the expressions. For example, the following expression in line 14 creates a string based on the values of the speed and vehicle variables.

```
{{speed + ' ' + vehicle}}
```

Another thing to note is that you can call functions in the scope from within an AngularJS expression. When the expression is evaluated, the back-end function is called and the return value is rendered to the view. You can pass variable names from the scope into a function, as well as numbers and strings, as illustrated in the following expression from line 19:

```
<a ng-click="setValues('Fast', newVehicle)">
```

The final thing to note is that the values assigned to the AngularJS attributes of the HTML elements are evaluated as AngularJS expressions even though they are not explicitly wrapped in {{}} brackets.

Figure 5.2 shows the rendered web page based on the expressions. Note that when the links of the page are clicked on, the resulting function calls adjust the scope, which changes how the previously discussed expressions are rendered.

Listing 5.3 **expressions_scope.js: Building a Scope That AngularJS Expressions Can Use**

```
01 angular.module('myApp', [])
02   .controller('myController', function($scope) {
03     $scope.speed = 'Slow';
04     $scope.vehicle = 'Train';
05     $scope.newSpeed = 'Hypersonic';
06     $scope.newVehicle = 'Plane';
07     $scope.upper = function(aString){
08       return angular.uppercase(aString);
09     };
10     $scope.lower = function(aString){
11       return angular.lowercase(aString);
12     };
13     $scope.setValues = function(speed, vehicle){
14       $scope.speed = speed;
15       $scope.vehicle = vehicle;
16     };
17   });
```

Listing 5.4 `expressions_scope.html`: An AngularJS Template That Uses Expressions in Various Ways to Interact with Data from the Scope Model

```
01 <!doctype html>
02 <html ng-app="myApp">
03   <head>
04     <title>AngularJS Expressions</title>
05     <style>
06       a{color: blue; text-decoration: underline; cursor: pointer}
07     </style>
08   </head>
09   <body>
10     <div ng-controller="myController">
11       Directly accessing variables in the scope:<br>
12       {{speed}} {{vehicle}}<hr>
13       Adding variables in the scope:<br>
14       {{speed + ' ' + vehicle}}<hr>
15       Calling function in the scope:<br>
16       {{lower(speed)}} {{upper('Jeep')}}<hr>
17       <a ng-click="setValues('Fast', newVehicle)">
18         Click to change to Fast {{newVehicle}}</a><hr>
19       <a ng-click="setValues(newSpeed, 'Rocket')">
20         Click to change to {{newSpeed}} Rocket</a><hr>
21       <a ng-click="vehicle='Car'">
22         Click to change the vehicle to a Car</a><hr>
23       <a ng-click="vehicle='Enhanced ' + vehicle">
24         Click to Enhance Vehicle</a><hr>
25     <script src="http://code.angularjs.org/1.3.0/angular.min.js"></script>
26     <script src="js/expressions_scope.js"></script>
27   </body>
28 </html>
```

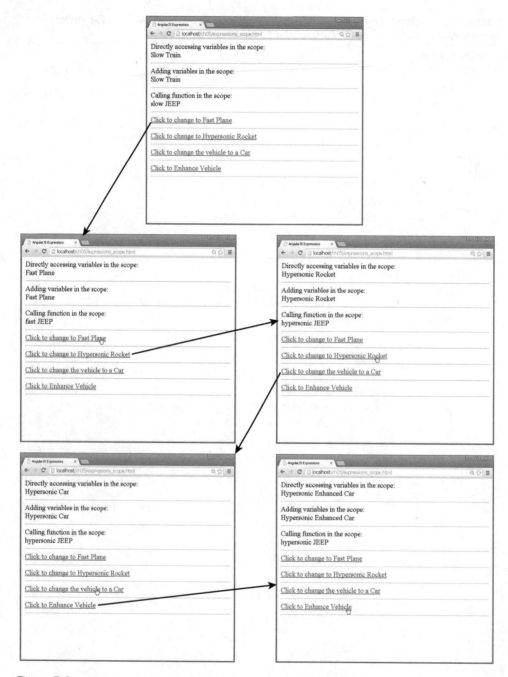

Figure 5.2   Using AngularJS expressions to represent and use scope data in the AngularJS view.

Using JavaScript in AngularJS Expressions

In this final example we take a look at some additional JavaScript interactions within the scope. As described previously, much of the JavaScript functionality is supported in AngularJS expression. To illustrate this better, the example shows some array manipulation as well as utilizing the JavaScript Math object within expressions.

Listing 5.5 creates a simple AngularJS controller that contains two arrays in the scope. Notice that on line 3, the following statement adds a Math variable to the scope by assigning it to windows.Math. This is necessary to use the JavaScript Math functionality because only the scope variables are available when AngularJS expressions are evaluated:

```
$scope.Math = window.Math;
```

Listing 5.6 implements an AngularJS template that uses AngularJS expressions to display the arrays, show the array length, as well as manipulate the array elements using push() and shift() directly in the expressions. Note that because we have added Math to the scope, we are able to use JavaScript Math operations directly in the expressions in lines 16 and 23.

Figure 5.3 shows the AngularJS web page rendered. Notice that as the links are clicked, the arrays get adjusted and the expressions are reevaluated.

Listing 5.5 `expressions_javascript.js`: Building a Scope with Arrays and the Math Object That AngularJS Expressions Can Use

```
01 angular.module('myApp', [])
02   .controller('myController', function($scope) {
03     $scope.Math = window.Math;
04     $scope.myArr = [1];
05     $scope.removedArr = [];
06   });
```

Listing 5.6 `expressions_javascript.html`: An AngularJS Template That Uses Expressions That Contain Arrays and Math Logic in Various Ways to Interact with Data from the Scope Model

```
01 <!doctype html>
02 <html ng-app="myApp">
03   <head>
04     <title>AngularJS Expressions</title>
05     <style>
06       a{color: blue; text-decoration: underline; cursor: pointer}
07     </style>
08   </head>
09   <body>
10     <div ng-controller="myController">
11       <h1>Expressions</h1>
12       Array:<br>
13         {{myArr}}<hr>
14       Elements removed from array:<br>
```

```
15          {{removedArr}}<hr>
16        <a ng-click="myArr.push(Math.floor(Math.random()*100 + 1))">
17          Click to append a value to the array</a><hr>
18        <a ng-click="removedArr.push(myArr.shift())">
19          Click to remove the first value from the array</a><hr>
20        Size of Array:<br>
21          {{myArr.length}}<hr>
22        Max number removed from the array:<br>
23          {{Math.max.apply(Math, removedArr)}}<hr>
24      <script src="http://code.angularjs.org/1.3.0/angular.min.js"></script>
25      <script src="js/expressions_javascript.js"></script>
26    </body>
27  </html>
```

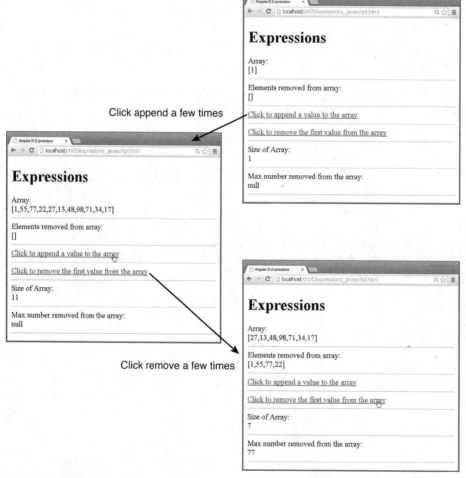

Figure 5.3   Using AngularJS expressions that apply JavaScript array and Math operations to interact with scope data.

Using Filters

A great feature of AngularJS is the capability to implement filters. Filters are a type of provider that hooks into the expression parser and modifies the results of the expression for display in a view—for example, to format time or currency values.

You implement filters inside expressions, using the following syntax:

```
{{ expression | filter}}
```

If you chain multiple filters together, they are executed in the order in which you specify them:

```
{{ expression | filter | filter }}
```

Some filters allow you to provide input in the form of function parameters. You add these parameters by using the following syntax:

```
{{ expression | filter:parameter1:parameter2 }}
```

Also, you can add filters, which are providers, to controllers and services by using dependency injection. The filter provider name is the name of the filter plus `Filter`. For example, the currency filter provider is named `currencyFilter`. The filter provider acts as a function, with the expression as the first parameter and any additional parameters after that. The following code defines a controller that injects `currencyFilter` and uses it to format results. Notice that `currencyFilter` is added to the dependency injection for the controller and is called as a function:

```
controller('myController', ['$scope', 'currencyFilter',
                        function($scope, myCurrencyFilter){
  $scope.getCurrencyValue = function(value){
    return myCurrencyFilter(value, "$USD");
  };
}]);
```

Using Built-in Filters

AngularJS provides several types of filters that enable you to easily format strings, objects, and arrays in AngularJS templates. Table 5.1 lists the built-in filters provided with AngularJS.

Table 5.1   **Filters That Modify Expressions in AngularJS Templates**

Filter	Description
currency[:symbol]	Formats a number as currency, based on the symbol value provided. If no symbol value is provided, the default symbol for the locale is used. For example: `{{123.46	currency:"$USD" }}`

Filter	Description
`filter:exp:compare`	Filters the expression with the value of the `exp` parameter, based on the value of `compare`. The `exp` parameter can be a string, an object, or a function. The `compare` parameter can be a function that accepts expected and actual values and returns `true` or `false`. The `compare` parameter can also be a Boolean, where `true` is a strict comparison of `actual===expected` or `false` is a relaxed comparison that checks whether the value is a subset of the actual value. For example: `{{"Some Text to Compare"	filter:"text":false`
`json`	Formats a JavaScript object into a JSON string. For example: `{{ {'name':'Brad'}	json }}`
`limitTo:limit`	Limits the data represented in the expression by the `limit` amount. If the expression is a `String`, it is limited by number of characters. If the result of the expression is an `Array`, it is limited by the number of elements. For example: `{{ ['a','b','c','d']	limitTo:2 }}`
`lowercase`	Outputs the result of the expression as lowercase.
`uppercase`	Outputs the result of the expression as uppercase.
`number[:fraction]`	Formats the number as text. If a `fraction` parameter is specified, the number of decimal places displayed is limited to that size. For example: `{{ 123.4567	number:3 }}`
`orderBy:exp:reverse`	Orders an array based on the `exp` parameter. The `exp` parameter can be a function that calculates the value of an item in the array or a string that specifies an object property in an array of objects. The `reverse` parameter is `true` for descending order or `false` for ascending.

Filter	Description
date[:*format*]	Formats a JavaScript `Date` object, a timestamp, or date ISO 8601 date strings, using the *format* parameter. For example: `{{1389323623006	date:'yyyy-MM-dd HH:mm:ss Z'}}`

The `format` parameter uses the following date formatting characters:

- yyyy: Four-digit year
- yy: Two-digit year since 2000
- MMMM: Month in year, `January–December`
- MMM: Month in year, `Jan–Dec`
- MM: Month in year, padded, `01–12`
- M: Month in year, `1–12`
- dd: Day in month, padded, `01–31`
- d: Day in month, `1–31`
- EEEE: Day in week, `Sunday–Saturday`
- EEE: Day in Week, `Sun–Sat`
- HH: Hour in day, padded, `00–23`
- H: Hour in day, `0–23`
- hh: Hour in am/pm, padded, `01–12`
- h: Hour in am/pm, `1–12`
- mm: Minute in hour, padded, `00–59`
- m: Minute in hour, `0–59`
- ss: Second in minute, padded, `00–59`
- s: Second in minute, `0–59`
- .sss or ,sss: Millisecond in second, padded, `000–999`
- a: am/pm marker
- Z: Four-digit time zone offset, `-1200–+1200`

The `format` string for `date` can also be one of the following predefined names. The format that follows is shown as `en_US` but will match the locale of the AngularJS application:

- medium: `'MMM d, y h:mm:ss a'`
- short: `'M/d/yy h:mm a'`
- fullDate: `'EEEE, MMMM d,y'`
- longDate: `'MMMM d, y'`
- mediumDate: `'MMM d, y'`
- shortDate: `'M/d/yy'`
- mediumTime: `'h:mm:ss a'`
- shortTime: `'h:mm a'`

Listings 5.7 and 5.8 show how to implement some basic filters in AngularJS. Listing 5.7 implements a controller with JSONObj, word, and days properties. Listing 5.8 implements number, currency, date, json, limitTo, uppercase, and lowercase filters directly in expressions in the template. Figure 5.4 shows the output of these listings.

Listing 5.7 **`filters.js`: Building a Scope That AngularJS Filters Can Use**

```
01 angular.module('myApp', [])
02   .controller('myController', function($scope) {
03     $scope.currentDate = new Date();
04     $scope.JSONObj = { title: "myTitle" };
05     $scope.word="Supercalifragilisticexpialidocious";
06     $scope.days=['Monday', 'Tuesday', 'Wednesday',
07                      'Thursday', 'Friday'];
08   });
```

Listing 5.8 **`filters.html`: An AngularJS Template That Implements Various Types of Filters to Modify Data Displayed in the Rendered View**

```
01 <!doctype html>
02 <html ng-app="myApp">
03   <head>
04     <title>AngularJS Filters</title>
05   </head>
06   <body>
07     <div ng-controller="myController">
08       <h2>Basic Filters</h2>
09       Number: {{123.45678|number:3}}<br>
10       Currency: {{123.45678|currency:"$"}}<br>
11       Date: {{ currentDate | date:'yyyy-MM-dd HH:mm:ss Z'}}<br>
12       JSON: {{ JSONObj | json }}<br>
13       Limit Array: {{ days | limitTo:3 }}<br>
14       Limit String: {{ word | limitTo:9 }}<br>
15       Uppercase: {{ word | uppercase | limitTo:9 }}<br>
16       Lowercase: {{ word | lowercase | limitTo:9 }}
17     <script src="http://code.angularjs.org/1.3.0/angular.min.js"></script>
18     <script src="js/filters.js"></script>
19   </body>
20 </html>
```

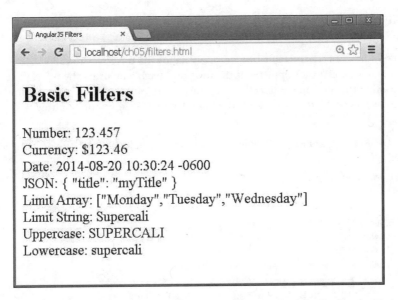

Figure 5.4   Using AngularJS filters to modify data before displaying it in the AngularJS view.

Using Filters to Implement Ordering and Filtering

A very common use of filters is to order or filter out dynamic elements built using the ng-repeat directive from JavaScript arrays. This section provides an example of implementing orderBy filters to generate a table that can be sorted by column and filtered by a string from an <input> element.

Listing 5.9 implements a controller that defines the $scope.planes array to use as input data in the scope. Since you do not want to alter the actual model data when sorting and filtering, line 12 adds the $scope.filteredPlanes property to store the filtered array.

Notice that line 13 sets a $scope.reverse value to keep track of the sort direction. Then line 14 sets a $scope.column value to keep track of which property name of objects in the planes array to sort on. Lines 15–16 define the setSort() function, which is used to update the column and reverse values.

Line 19 defines the $scope.filterString property, which filters the objects to include in filteredPlanes. Lines 20–23 define the setFilter() function, which calls the filterFilter() provider to limit the items in filteredPlanes to the ones that loosely match filterString. Lines 2 and 3 inject the filterFilter provider into the controller.

Listing 5.10 implements a template that includes a text `<input>` that binds to the `filterString` value and a button `<input>` that calls `setFilter()` when clicked.

Notice that in lines 14–16 the table headers apply `ng-click` directives to call `setSort()` to set the sort column. Lines 18–23 implement the rows of the table by using the `ng-repeat` directive. Notice that the `ng-repeat` directive uses the `orderBy` filter to specify the column name and reverse values set by the `setSort()` function. Figure 5.5 shows the resulting web page.

Listing 5.9   **`filter_sort.js`: Building a Scope That AngularJS Can Use and Then Sorting and Ordering**

```
01  angular.module('myApp', [])
02    .controller('myController', ['$scope', 'filterFilter',
03                               function($scope, filterFilter) {
04      $scope.planes = [
05        {make: 'Boeing', model: '777', capacity: 440},
06        {make: 'Boeing', model: '747', capacity: 700},
07        {make: 'Airbus', model: 'A380', capacity: 850},
08        {make: 'Airbus', model: 'A340', capacity: 420},
09        {make: 'McDonnell Douglas', model: 'DC10', capacity: 380},
10        {make: 'McDonnell Douglas', model: 'MD11', capacity: 410},
11        {make: 'Lockheed', model: 'L1011', capacity: 380}];
12      $scope.filteredPlanes = $scope.planes;
13      $scope.reverse = true;
14      $scope.column = 'make';
15      $scope.setSort = function(column){
16        $scope.column = column;
17        $scope.reverse = !$scope.reverse;
18      };
19      $scope.filterString = '';
20      $scope.setFilter = function(value){
21        $scope.filteredPlanes =
22          filterFilter($scope.planes, $scope.filterString);
23      };
24    }]);
```

Listing 5.10 **filter_sort.html**: An AngularJS Template That Implements **filter** and **orderBy** Filters to Order and Filter Items in a Table View

```
01 <!doctype html>
02 <html ng-app="myApp">
03   <head>
04     <title>AngularJS Sorting and Filtering</title>
05     <style>
06       table{text-align:right;}
07       td,th{padding:3px;}
08       th{cursor:pointer;}
09     </style>
10   </head>
11   <body>
12     <div ng-controller="myController">
13       <h2>Sorting and Filtering</h2>
14       <input type="text" ng-model="filterString">
15       <input type="button" ng-click="setFilter()" value="Filter">
16       <table>
17       <tr>
18         <th ng-click="setSort('make')">Make</th>
19         <th ng-click="setSort('model')">Model</th>
20         <th ng-click="setSort('capacity')">Capacity</th>
21       </tr>
22       <tr ng-repeat=
23           "plane in filteredPlanes | orderBy:column:reverse">
24         <td>{{plane.make}}</td>
25         <td>{{plane.model}}</td>
26         <td>{{plane.capacity}}</td>
27       </tr>
28       </table>
29       <script src="http://code.angularjs.org/1.3.0/angular.min.js"></script>
30       <script src="js/filter_sort.js"></script>
31   </body>
32 </html>
```

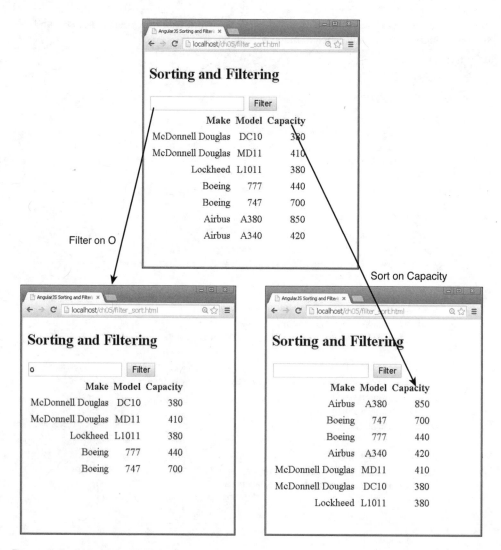

Figure 5.5   Using AngularJS filters to filter and order items in a table in the AngularJS view.

Creating Custom Filters

AngularJS enables you to create your own custom filter provider and then use it in expressions, controllers, and services as if it were a built-in filter. AngularJS provides the `filter()` method to create a filter provider and register it with the dependency injector server.

The `filter()` method accepts a name for the filter as the first argument and a function for the second argument. The filter function should accept the expression input as the first parameter and any additional parameters following that. For example:

```
filter('myFilter', function(){
  return function(input, param1, param2){
    return <<modified input>>;
  };
});
```

Inside the filter function you can change the value of the input any way you like. Whatever value is returned from the filter function is returned as the expression results.

Listings 5.11 and 5.12 create a custom filter function that censors words from a string and allows for a replacement value as an optional parameter. Listing 5.11 implements the `censor` filter provider in lines 2–11. Then in lines 12–20 the controller adds the `censorFilter` provider, using dependency injection. The `fitlerText()` function in lines 17–19 utilizes the `censorFilter` provider to censor text and replace it with `<<censored>>`.

The code in Listing 5.12 implements a template that utilizes the filter in a couple of ways, including calling `filterText()` based on a click event. Notice in line 9 that the value passed to the `censor` filter comes from the variable `censorText` in the scope. Figure 5.6 shows the output of these listings.

Listing 5.11 `filter_customer.js`: Implementing a Custom Filter Provider in AngularJS

```
01 angular.module('myApp', [])
02   .filter('censor', function() {
03     return function(input, replacement) {
04       var cWords = ['bad', 'evil', 'dark'];
05       var out = input;
06       for(var i=0; i<cWords.length; i++){
07         out = out.replace(cWords[i], replacement);
08       }
09       return out;
10     };
11   })
12   .controller('myController', ['$scope', 'censorFilter',
13                                function($scope, myCensorFilter) {
14     $scope.censorText = "***";
15     $scope.phrase="This is a bad phrase.";
16     $scope.txt = "Click to filter out dark and evil.";
17     $scope.filterText = function(){
18       $scope.txt = myCensorFilter($scope.txt, '<<censored>>');
19     };
20   }]);
```

Listing 5.12 **`filter_custom.html`: An AngularJS Template That Uses a Custom Filter**

```
01 <!doctype html>
02 <html ng-app="myApp">
03   <head>
04     <title>AngularJS Custom Filter</title>
05   </head>
06   <body>
07     <div ng-controller="myController">
08       <h2>Sorting and Filtering</h2>
09       {{phrase | censor:censorText}}<br>
10       {{"This is some bad, dark, evil text." | censor:"happy"}}
11       <p ng-click="filterText()">{{txt}}</p>
12     <script src="http://code.angularjs.org/1.3.0/angular.min.js"></script>
13     <script src="js/filter_custom.js"></script>
14   </body>
15 </html>
```

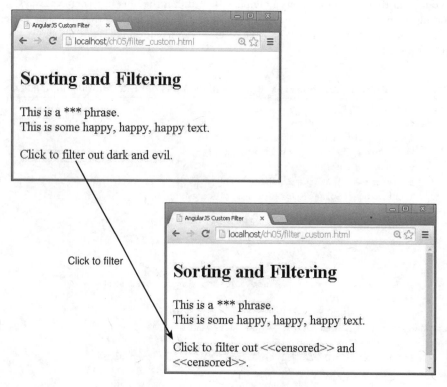

Figure 5.6   Creating and using custom filters in an AngularJS view.

Summary

AngularJS templates are simple to implement yet very powerful and extensive. This chapter discusses the components of AngularJS templates and how they work together to extend HTML DOM behavior and functionality. Expressions are bits of JavaScript code contained in {{ }} brackets or within directive definitions in the AngularJS template. Expressions have access to the scope, so you can render scope values to the view.

Filters act as modifiers to expressions and enable you to format expression results for specific purposes. AngularJS provides several built-in filters, such as for currency and date formatting. You can also create your own custom filters that provide any formatting or modifications you want apply before rendering data to the page. You inject filters as providers into the injector service and can therefore access them inside controllers and templates, using dependency injection. This means you have access to filters within your JavaScript code as well.

Implementing Directives in AngularJS Views

One of the most powerful features of AngularJS is directives. Directives extend the behavior of HTML, enabling you to create custom HTML elements, attributes, and classes with functionality specific to an application. AngularJS provides several built-in directives. In fact, the majority of the AngularJS library is built-in directives. These directives provide the capability to interact with form elements, bind data in the scope to the view, and interact with browser events.

This chapter discusses the built-in directives and how to implement them in AngularJS templates. You will learn how to apply these directives in your AngularJS templates and support them in the back-end controllers to quickly turn the rendered view into an interactive application.

Understanding Directives

Directives are a combination of AngularJS template markups and supporting JavaScript code. AngularJS directive markups can be HTML attributes, element names, or CSS classes. The JavaScript directive code defines the template data and behavior of the HTML elements.

The AngularJS compiler traverses the template DOM and compiles all directives. Then it links the directives by combining a directive with a scope to produce a new live view. The live view contains the DOM elements and functionality defined in the directive.

Using Built-in Directives

Most of the AngularJS functionality that you need to implement in HTML elements is provided in the built-in directives. These directives are provided by the library and are available when the AngularJS JavaScript library is loaded.

Directives provide a wide variety of support for AngularJS applications. The following sections describe most of the AngularJS directives, which fall into the following categories:

- Directives that support AngularJS functionality
- Directives that extend form elements
- Directives that bind the page elements to values in the scope model
- Directives that bind page events to controllers

Each of the following sections includes a table containing the related directives along with a basic description. You do not need to understand all of these directives right now; the tables are there more for references. Subsequent sections and chapters provide sample code for using many of these directives.

Directives That Support AngularJS Functionality

Several directives provide support for AngularJS functionality. These directives do everything from bootstrapping an application to ensuring that Boolean expressions that AngularJS requires are preserved in the DOM.

Table 6.1 lists these directives and describes the behavior and usage of each.

Table 6.1   Directives That Support AngularJS Template Functionality

Directive	Description
ngApp	This directive is used to bootstrap an application to a root element. This attribute is set to the name of the AngularJS module to use as the application root, and the HTML element that contains it acts as the compilation root for the template. For example, the following sets module myApp as the application in the `<html>` element: `<html ng-app="myApp">`
ngCloak	When this attribute is present in an element, that element is not displayed until after the AngularJS template has been fully compiled. Otherwise, the raw form of the element with the template code is displayed.
ngController	This directive attaches a controller to this element in the view to create a new scope, as described in earlier chapters. For example: `<div ng-controller="myController">`
ngHref	This is an option you can use instead of using the href attribute, which might be broken if the user clicks the link before the expression has been evaluated if you include template syntax such as {{hash}}.

Directive	Description
ngInclude	This directive automatically fetches, compiles, and includes an external HTML fragment from the server. Using it is a great way to include partial HTML data from server-side scripts. For example: `<div ng-include="/info/sidebar.html">`
ngList	This directive converts an `Array` object in the scope into a delimiter-separated string. (Comma is the default delimiter.) For example, if the scope contains an array named `items`, the displayed value in the following `<input>` would be `item1, item2, item3,...`: `<input ng-model="items" ng-list=",">`
ngNonBindable	When this directive is present in an element, AngularJS does not compile or bind the contents of the element during compilation. This is useful if you are trying to display code in the element. For example: `<p ng-non-bindable>Expression Syntax: {{exp}}</p>`
ngOpen	Browsers are not required to preserve Boolean attributes of elements. If this attribute is present, it is `true`. This directive enables you to preserve the `true`/`false` state of an element by testing the existence of the attribute. For example, the following applies `ngOpen` based on the `open` value in the scope: `<details ng-open="open">`

ngPluralize	This directive enables you to display messages according to the `en-US` localization rules bundled with AngularJS. You can configure `ngPluralize` by adding the `count` and `when` attributes, as shown here:
	
	`<p ng-pluralize count="itemCount"`
	`    when="{'0': 'Cart is empty.',`
	`          'one': 'Purchase 1 item.',`
	`          'other': 'Purchase {{itemCount}} items.'}">`
	`</p>`

ngReadonly	Similar to `ngOpen` but for the `readonly` Boolean value. For example, the following applies `ngReadonly` based on the `notChangeable` value in the scope: `<input type="text" ng-readonly="notChangeable">`
ngRequired	This directive is similar to `ngOpen` but for the `required` Boolean value for `<input>` elements in a form. For example, the following applies `ngRequired` based on the required value in the scope: `<input type="text" ng-required="required">`

ngSelected	This directive is similar to `ngOpen` but for the `selected` Boolean value. For example, the following applies `ngSelected` based on the selected value in the scope:
	
	`<option id="optionA" ng-selected="selected">`
	`  Option A`
	`</option>`

Directive	Description
ngSrc	You can use this directive instead of using the `src` attribute, which is broken until the expression has been evaluated, if you include template syntax such as `{{username}}`. For example: `<img ng-src="/images/{{username}}/test.jpg" />`
ngSrcset	You can use this directive instead of using the `srcset` attribute, which is broken before the expression has been evaluated. For example: `<img ng-srcset="/images/{{username}}/test.jpg 2x" />`
ngTransclude	This directive marks the element as the transclude point for directives that use the transclude option to wrap other elements.
ngView	This directive includes a rendered template of the current route into the main layout file. Routes are discussed in Chapter 9.
script	This directive loads the content of a `script` tag with `next/ng-template` so that it can be used by `ngInclude`, `ngView`, or other template directives.

The directives in Table 6.1 are used in different ways in various parts of the code. You have already seen a few of them such as `ngApp` and `ngController` used in previous examples. Some are fairly intuitive, such as using `ng-src` instead of `src` when implementing `<img>` elements in a template. Others will be used in various examples in subsequent chapters.

I did want to give you an example at this point of using the `ngInclude` directive. This little directive is simple to employ and can be used for a variety of purposes, especially if you are trying to introduce AngularJS into an existing system. In this example we will use `ngInclude` to swap the banner bar at the top of a basic web page by loading different partial HTML files from the server.

The code in Listing 6.1 implements a very basic AngularJS controller that stores an HTML filename in a variable named `titleBar`. The code in Listing 6.2 implements an AngularJS template that includes a couple of links at the top to switch pages and a `<div>` element on line 24 that using `ng-include` to change the contents of the div to the file specified by `titleBar`.

The different versions of the title bar are located in the files shown in Listings 6.3 and 6.4. Basically, these files just contain a `<p>` element that has either the `large` or `small` class assigned to it. The class definitions are located in the `<style>` element of Listing 6.2.

Figure 6.1 shows the two title banners. When the links are clicked to switch banners, the contents of the `<div>` element in the original are replaced by the new HTML file being loaded.

Listing 6.1 `directive_angular_include.js`: Implementing a Controller to Store the HTML Filename for a Title Element in the Scope

```
01 angular.module('myApp', []).
02   controller('myController', function($scope) {
03     $scope.titleBar = "small_title.html";
04   });
```

Listing 6.2 `directive_angular_include.html`: An AngularJS Template That Uses the `nd-include` Directive to Change the Title Bar of the Page by Swapping between Two HTML Files

```
01 <!doctype html>
02 <html ng-app="myApp">
03 <head>
04   <title>AngularJS Data Include Directive</title>
05   <style>
06     .large{
07       background-color: blue; color: white;
08       text-align: center;
09       font: bold 50px/80px verdana, serif;
10       border: 6px black ridge; }
11     .small{
12       background-color: lightgrey;
13       text-align: center;
14       border: 1px black solid; }
15     a{
16       color: blue; text-decoration: underline;
17       cursor: pointer; }
18   </style>
19 </head>
20 <body>
21   <div ng-controller="myController">
22     [<a ng-click="titleBar='large_title.html'">Make Title Large</a>]
23     [<a ng-click="titleBar='small_title.html'">Make Title Small</a>]
24     <div ng-include="titleBar"></div>
25   </div>
26   <script src="http://code.angularjs.org/1.3.0/angular.min.js"></script>
27   <script src="js/directive_angular_include.js"></script>
28 </body>
29 </html>
```

Listing 6.3   **small_title.html: A Partial HTML File That Contains the Small Version of the Title**

```
01 <p class="small">
02    This is a Small Title
03 </p>
```

Listing 6.4   **large_title.html: A Partial HTML File That Contains the Large Version of the Title**

```
01 <p class="large">
02    This is a Large Title
03 </p>?
```

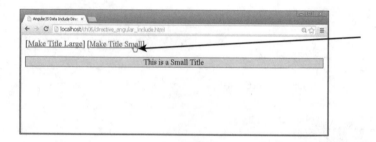

Figure 6.1   Using the ng-include directive to dynamically change the view using different HTML partial files.

Directives That Extend Form Elements

AngularJS is heavily integrated with form elements to provide data binding and event binding for form elements in applications. To provide AngularJS functionality in the correct way, form elements are extended when compiled.

Table 6.2 lists the form elements that AngularJS extends.

Table 6.2   **Directives That Extend Form Elements to Support AngularJS Template Functionality**

Directive	Description
a	This directive modifies the default behavior to prevent the default action when the `href` attribute is empty. This enables you to create action links by using `ngClick` or other event directives. For example: `<a href="" ng-click="handleClick()">Click Me</a>`

form/ngForm	AngularJS allows forms to be nested for validation purposes such that a form is valid when all child forms are valid as well. However, browsers do not allow nesting of `<form>` elements; therefore, you should use `<ng-form>` instead. For example:
	
	`<ng-form name="myForm">`
	  `<input type="text" ng-model="myName" required>`
	`</ng-form>`

input	You can modify this directive to provide the following additional AngularJS attributes: ■ `ngModel`: Binds the value of this input to a variable in the scope. ■ `name`: Specifies the name of the form. ■ `required`: When present, a value is required for this field. ■ `ngRequired`: Sets the required attribute based on the evaluation of the `ngRequired` expression. ■ `ngMinlength`: Sets the `minlength` validation error amount. ■ `ngMaxlength`: Sets the `maxlength` validation error amount. ■ `ngPattern`: Specifies a `regex` pattern to match the input value against for validation. ■ `ngChange`: Specifies an expression to be executed when the input changes—for example, executing a function in the scope.
input.checkbox	This directive adds the following extra AngularJS attributes in addition to those already provided with `input`: ■ `ngTrueValue`: Sets a value in the scope when the element is checked. ■ `ngFalseValue`: Sets a value in the model when the element is not checked.

Directive	Description
`input.email`	This directive is the same as `input`.
`input.number`	This directive adds the following extra AngularJS attributes in addition to those already provided to `input`: • `min`: Sets the `min` validation error amount. • `max`: Sets the `max` validation error amount.
`input.radio`	This directive adds the following extra AngularJS attribute in addition to those already provided to `input`: • `value`: Sets a value in the scope when the element is selected.
`input.text`	This directive is the same as `input`.
`input.url`	This directive is the same as `input`.
`input.date`	This directive adds date validation and transformation for date input elements. The value in the scope model must also be a JavaScript `Date` object. This directive adds the following extra AngularJS attributes in addition to those already provided to `input`: • `min`: Sets the `min` date validation error amount. • `max`: Sets the `max` date validation error amount.
`input.dateTimeLocal`	This directive is the same as `input.date` except that the format must be entered as a valid ISO-8601 local date-time format (yyyy-MM-ddTHH:mm). For example: `2014-11-28T12:37`
`input.month`	This directive is the same as `input.date` except that the format must be entered as a valid ISO-8601 month format (yyyy-MM). For example: `2014-11`
`input.time`	This directive is the same as `input.date` except that the format must be entered as a valid ISO-8601 time format (HH:mm). For example: `12:37`
`input.week`	This directive is the same as `input.date` except that the format must be entered as a valid ISO-8601 week format (yyyy-W##). For example: `2014-W02`
`select`	This directive adds the additional `ngOptions` directive to the `<select>` element.

Directive	Description

ngOptions	This directive enables you to add options based on an iterative expression. If the data source in the scope is an array, use the following expressions for ngOptions to set the label, name, and value attributes of each <option> element in the <select>:
	
	`label for value in array`
	`select as label for value in array`
	`label group by group for value in array`
	`select as label group by group for value in array track by trackexpr`
	
	If the source for ngOptions in the scope is a JavaScript object, use the following expression syntax:
	
	`label for (key , value) in object`
	`select as label for (key , value) in object`
	`label group by group for (key, value) in object`
	`select as label group by group for (key, value) in object`
	
	For example:
	`<select ng-model="color"`
	`        ng-options="c.name for c in colors">`
	`  <option value="">-- choose color --</option>`
	`</select>`

textarea	This directive is the same as input.

Listings 6.5 and 6.6 implement some basic AngularJS form element integration with the scope. Listing 6.5 initializes the scope. Listing 6.6 implements several common form components, including a text box, a check box, radio buttons, and a select element to illustrate how they are defined in the template and interact with data in the scope. Figure 6.2 shows the resulting web page.

Listing 6.5 `directive_form.js`: Implementing a Controller for Form Directives

```
01 angular.module('myApp', []).
02    controller('myController', function($scope) {
03       $scope.cameras = [
04          {make:'Canon', model:'70D', mp:20.2},
05          {make:'Canon', model:'6D', mp:20},
06          {make:'Nikon', model:'D7100', mp:24.1},
07          {make:'Nikon', model:'D5200', mp:24.1}];
08       $scope.cameraObj=$scope.cameras[0];
09       $scope.cameraName = 'Canon';
10       $scope.cbValue = '';
11       $scope.someText = '';
12    });
```

Listing 6.6 `directive_form.html`: An AngularJS Template That Implements Several Different Form Element Directives

```
01 <!doctype html>
02 <html ng-app="myApp">
03 <head>
04   <title>AngularJS Form Directives</title>
05 </head>
06 <body>
07   <div ng-controller="myController">
08     <h2>Forms Directives</h2>
09     <input type="text" ng-model="someText"> {{someText}}<hr>
10     <input type="checkbox" ng-model="cbValue"
11           ng-true-value="AWESOME" ng-false-value="BUMMER">
12     Checkbox: {{cbValue}}<hr>
13     <input type="radio"
14       ng-model="cameraName" value="Canon"> Canon<br/>
15     <input type="radio"
16       ng-model="cameraName" value="Nikon"> Nikon<br/>
17     Selected Camera: {{cameraName}} <hr>
18     <select ng-model="camera"
19       ng-options="c.model group by c.make for c in cameras">
20     </select>
21     {{camera|json}}
22   <script src="http://code.angularjs.org/1.3.0/angular.min.js"></script>
23   <script src="js/directive_form.js"></script>
24 </body>
25 </html>
```

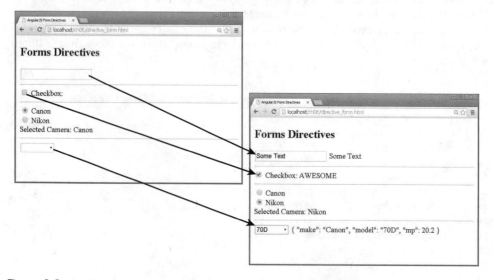

Figure 6.2   Implementing form directive elements in AngularJS template views.

Directives That Bind the Model to Page Elements

AngularJS templates enable you to bind data in the scope directly to what is displayed in HTML elements. You can bind data to the view in several ways, including these:

- **Value:** You can directly represent the value of a form element in the scope. For example, a text input can be a `String` variable in the scope, but a check box would be represented by a `Boolean` value.

- **HTML:** You can represent the value of data in the scope in the HTML output of an element by using expressions such as this:

  `<p>{{myTitle}}</p>`

- **Attributes:** The value of HTML element attributes can reflect the data in the scope by using expressions in the definition such as this:

  `<a ng-href="/{{hash}}/index.html">{{hash}}</a>`.

- **Visibility:** The visibility of an element can reflect the scope in the view. For example, when an expression based on the scope is `true`, the element is visible; otherwise, it is invisible.

- **Existence:** You can omit elements from the compiled DOM, based on values in the scope.

Table 6.3 lists the directives that bind the data in the scope directly to elements in the view.

Table 6.3   **Directives That Bind Data in the Scope to the Value, Expressions, Visibility, and Existence of HTML Elements**

Directive	Description
ngBind	This directive tells AngularJS to replace the `text` content of the HTML element with the value of a given expression and also to update the `text` content if the value in the scope changes. For example: `<span ng-bind="titleString"></span>`
ngBindHtml	This directive tells AngularJS to replace the `innerHTML` content of the HTML element with the value of a given expression and also to update the `innerHTML` content if the value in the scope changes. For example: `<div ng-bind-html="someHTML"></div>`

ngBindTemplate	This directive is similar to `ngBind` except that the expression can contain multiple `{{}}` expression blocks. For example:
	`<span`
	`  ng-bind-template="{{aValue}} and {{anotherValue}}">`
	`</span>`

Directive	Description
ngClass	This directive dynamically sets the CSS class of the element by data binding an expression that represents the classes to be added. When the value of the expression changes, the CSS classes of the element are automatically updated. For example: `<p ng-class="myPStyles"></p>`

ngClassEven	This directive is the same as ngClass except that it works with ngRepeat to apply the class changes only to even indexed elements in the set. For example:
	
	`<li ng-repeat="item in items">`
	`  <span ng-class-even="evenRowClass">{{item}}</span>`
	`</li>`

ngClassOdd	This directive is the same as ngClass except that it works with ngRepeat to apply the class changes only to odd indexed elements in the set. For example:
	
	`<li ng-repeat="item in items">`
	`  <span ng-class-odd="oddRowClass">{{item}}</span>`
	`</li>`

ngDisabled	This directive disables a button element if the expression evaluates to true.
ngHide	This directive shows or hides the HTML element based on the expression provided, using the .ng-hide CSS class provided in AngularJS. If the expression evaluates to false in the scope, the element is displayed; otherwise, it is hidden. For example: `<div ng-hide="myValue"></div>`
ngShow	This directive is the same as ngHide except in reverse: If the expression evaluates to true in the scope, the element is displayed; otherwise, it is hidden. For example: `<div ng-show="myValue"></div>`
ngIf	This directive deletes or re-creates a portion of the DOM tree, based on the expression. This is different from show or hide because the HTML does not show up at all in the DOM. For example: `<div ng-if="present"> </div>`
ngModel	This directive binds the value of an `<input>`, `<select>`, or `<textarea>` element to a value in the scope model. When the user changes the value of the element, the value is automatically changed in the scope and vice versa. For example: `<input type="text" ng-model="myString">`

Directive	Description
ngRepeat	This directive enables you to add multiple HTML elements based on an array in the scope. This is extremely useful for lists, tables, and menus. ngRepeat uses the item in collections style of iteration syntax. A new scope is created for each individual HTML element created. During the looping to generate the HTML elements, the following variables are visible in the scope: • $index: An iterator index based on 0 for the first element. • $first: A Boolean that is true if this is the first element. • $middle: A Boolean that is true if this is not the first or last element. • $last: A Boolean that is true if this is the last element. • $even: A Boolean that is true if the iterator is even. • $odd: A Boolean that is true if the iterator is odd. For example, the following iterates and builds a series of `<li>` elements based on an array of users with a firstname property: ```<li ng-repeat="user in users">` ` {{$index}}: {{user.firstname}}</li>```
ngInit	This directive is used with ngRepeat to initialize a value during the iteration. For example: ```<div ng-repeat="user in users" ng-init="offset=21">` ` {{$index+offset}}: {{user.firstname}}</div>```
ngStyle	This directive enables you to set the style dynamically, based on an object in the scope where the property names and values match CSS attributes. For example: ```<span ng-style="myStyle">Stylized Text</span>```
ngSwitch	This directive enables you to dynamically swap which DOM element to include in the compiled template, based on a scope expression. The following is an example of the syntax used for multiple elements: ```<div ng-switch="myLocation">` ` <div ng-switch-when="home">Home Info</div>` ` <div ng-switch-when="work">Work Info</div>` ` <div ng-switch-default>Default Info</div>` `</div>```
ngValue	This directive binds the selected value of an input[select] or input[radio] to the expression specified in ngModel. For example: ```<div ng-repeat="pizza in pizzas"` ` <input type="radio" name="pizza"` ` ng-model="myPizza" ng-value="pizza" id="{{pizza}}" >` `</div>```

Listings 6.7 and 6.8 provide some examples of basic AngularJS binding directives. Listing 6.7 initializes the scope values, including the mystyle object in line 4. Listing 6.8 provides the actual implementation of the binding directives in the template.

With only a few exceptions, the template code in Listing 6.8 is straightforward. Lines 15 and 16 bind the radio button <input> to the myStyle['background-color'] property in the scope. This illustrates how to handle style names that do not allow the dot notation that's usually used (for example, myStyle.color). Also note that the value of the radio buttons is set using ng-value to get the color value from the ng-repeat scope.

Also note that when you set the class name using ng-class-even, the class name even needs to be in single quotes because it is a string. Figure 6.3 shows the resulting web page.

Listing 6.7   `directive_bind.js`: Implementing a Controller with a Scope Model to Support Data Binding Directives

```
01 angular.module('myApp', []).
02   controller('myController', function($scope) {
03     $scope.colors=['red','green','blue'];
04     $scope.myStyle = { "background-color": 'blue' };
05     $scope.days=['Monday', 'Tuesday', 'Wednesday',
06                     'Thursday', 'Friday'];
07     $scope.msg="Dynamic Message from the model";
08   });
```

Listing 6.8   `directive_bind.html`: An AngularJS Template That Implements Several Different Data Binding Directives

```
01 <!doctype html>
02 <html ng-app="myApp">
03 <head>
04   <title>AngularJS Data Binding Directives</title>
05   <style>
06     .even{background-color:lightgrey;}
07     .rect{display:inline-block; height:40px; width:100px;}
08   </style>
09 </head>
10 <body>
11   <div ng-controller="myController">
12     <h2>Data Binding Directives</h2>
13     <label ng-repeat="color in colors">
14       {{color}}
15       <input type="radio" ng-model="myStyle['background-color']"
16             ng-value="color" id="{{color}}" name="mColor">
17     </label>
18     <span class="rect" ng-style="myStyle"></span><hr>
19     <li ng-repeat="day in days">
```

```
20        <span ng-class-even="'even'">{{day}}</span>
21    </li><hr>
22    Show Message: <input type="checkbox" ng-model="checked" />
23    <p ng-if="checked" ng-bind="msg"> </p>
24 </div>
25 <script src="http://code.angularjs.org/1.3.0/angular.min.js"></script>
26 <script src="js/directive_bind.js"></script>
27 </body>
28 </html>
```

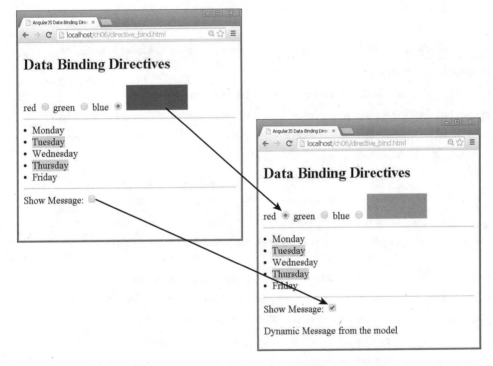

Figure 6.3   Implementing data binding directives in AngularJS template views.

Directives That Bind Page Events to Controllers

AngularJS templates enable you to bind browser events to controller code. This means you can handle user input from the scope's perspective. You can then implement handlers for browser events directly to the appropriate scope. The event directive works very much like the normal browser event handlers, except that they are directly linked to the scope context.

Table 6.4 lists the directives that bind page and device events to the AngularJS model. Each of these directives enables you to specify an expression, which is typically a function defined in the scope, as discussed in Chapter 5, "Using AngularJS Templates to Create Views." For example, the following is a function named `setTitle` in the scope:

```
$scope.setTitle = function(title){
  $scope.title = title;
};
```

You can bind the `setTitle()` function in the scope directly to an input button in the view by using the following `ng-click` directive:

```
<input type="button" ng-click="setTitle('New Title')">
```

Table 6.4   Directives That Bind Page/Device Events to AngularJS Model Functionality

Directive	Description
ngBlur	Evaluates an expression when the blur event is triggered.
ngChange	Evaluates an expression when the value of a form element is changed.
ngChecked	Evaluates an expression when a check box or radio element is checked.
ngClick	Evaluates an expression when the mouse is clicked.
ngCopy	Evaluates an expression when the copy event is triggered.
ngCut	Evaluates an expression when the cut event is triggered.
ngDblclick	Evaluates an expression when the mouse is double-clicked.
ngFocus	Evaluates an expression when the focus event is triggered by the element coming into focus.
ngKeydown	Evaluates an expression when a keyboard key is pressed.
ngKeypress	Evaluates an expression when a keyboard key is pressed and released.
ngKeyup	Evaluates an expression when a keyboard key is released.
ngMousedown	Evaluates an expression when a mouse key is pressed.
ngMouseenter	Evaluates an expression when the mouse enters the element.
ngMouseleave	Evaluates an expression when the mouse leaves the element.
ngMousemove	Evaluates an expression when the mouse cursor moves.
ngMouseover	Evaluates an expression when the mouse hovers over an element.
ngMouseup	Evaluates an expression when the mouse button is released.
ngPaste	Evaluates an expression when the paste event is triggered.

Directive	Description
ngSubmit	Prevents the default form submit action, which sends a request to the server and instead evaluates the specified expression.
ngSwipeLeft	Evaluates an expression when the swipe left event is triggered.
ngSwiteRight	Evaluates an expression when the swipe right event is triggered.

You can pass the JavaScript Event object into the event expressions by using the $event keyword. This enables you to access information about the event as well as stop propagation and everything else you normally can do with a JavaScript Event object. For example, the following ng-click directive passes the mouse click event to the myClick() handler function:

```
<input type="button" ng-click="myClick($event)">
```

The following sections provide some examples of using the AngularJS event directives to interact with events coming from the browser.

Using the Focus and Blur Events

The AngularJS ngBlur and ngFocus directives are useful to track when form elements go in and out of focus. For example, you might want to execute some code in the controller when a particular input element goes in and out of focus—say, to manipulate the input before updating the model. The code in Listings 6.9 and 6.10 illustrate an example of using the ngBlur and ngFocus directives to set values in the scope based on entering and leaving text inputs.

The code in Listing 6.9 implements a controller that defines an inputData object to store the values from two <input> elements. The focusGained() function will be called when an input comes into focus and will use the input parameter to set the value for that input in inputData to an empty string. The focusLost() function will accept the event and the input as inputs and will use the event object to get the value of the target element and update the corresponding property in inputData.

The code in Listing 6.10 is an AngularJS template that implements the two <input> elements and assigns the focusGained() and focusLost() handlers to the ng-focus and ng-blur attributes. Figure 6.4 shows the basic example in action. Note that when you click on an input element the value stored in inputData is set to an empty string, and when you leave the input element the value is updated.

Listing 6.9 `directive_focus_events.js`: Implementing a Controller with Scope Data and Event Handlers to Support Blur and Focus Events from the View

```
01 angular.module('myApp', []).
02   controller('myController', function($scope) {
03     $scope.inputData = { input1: '',
04                          input2: '' };
05     $scope.focusGained = function(input){
06       $scope.inputData[input] = '';
07     };
08     $scope.focusLost = function(event, input){
09       var element = angular.element(event.target);
10       var value = element.val();
11       $scope.inputData[input] = value.toUpperCase();
12     };
13   });
```

Listing 6.10 `directive_focus_events.html`: An AngularJS Template That Implements the `ngFocus` and `ngBlur` Directives

```
01 <!doctype html>
02 <html ng-app="myApp">
03 <head>
04   <title>AngularJS Focus Event Directives</title>
05 </head>
06 <body>
07   <div ng-controller="myController">
08     <h2>Focus Event Directives</h2>
09     Input 1:<br>
10     <input type="text"
11       ng-blur="focusLost($event, 'input1')"
12       ng-focus="focusGained('input1')"><br>
13     Input 2:<br>
14     <input type="text"
15       ng-blur="focusLost($event, 'input2')"
16       ng-focus="focusGained('input2')"><hr>
17     Input Data: {{inputData|json}}<br/>
18   </div>
19   <script src="http://code.angularjs.org/1.3.0/angular.min.js"></script>
20   <script src="js/directive_focus_events.js"></script>
21 </body>
22 </html>
```

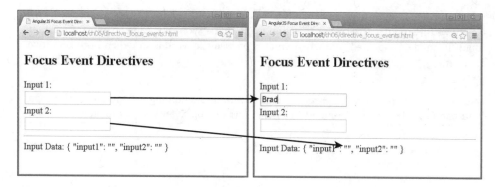

While typing Input Data is not updated

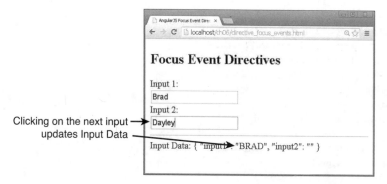

Clicking on the next input →
updates Input Data

Figure 6.4   Implementing focus event directives in AngularJS template views.

Handling Keyboard Events on AngularJS Elements

The most common keyboard event directives that you will use are the ngKeydown and ngKeyup events that are triggered when a keyboard key is pressed and released, respectively. Keyboard events are useful for interacting more closely with users as they type on the keyboard. Probably the most common keyboard interaction is to apply some action when a user presses the Enter key on the keyboard. The code in Listings 6.11 and 6.12 illustrate the usage of the ngKeydown and ngKeyup directives.

The code in Listing 6.11 implements a controller that provides the model and keyboard handler functions for the key-down and key-up events. The storedString variable is used to store the value of a text input whenever the user presses Enter while typing in the input. The keyInfo variable stores the keyCode for the last key pressed, and the keyStrokes array records the previous keyCodes for keys pressed. Inside the keyPressed() function, we check to see whether the keyCode is 13, meaning Enter was pressed, and if so we record the storedString and reset the other variables.

The code in Listing 6.12 is the AngularJS template that assigns the ng-keydown and ng-keyup directives to an <input> element. When ng-keydown is triggered the keyState variable in the scope is updated, and when `ng-keyup` is triggered the `keyPressed()` handler is called. Figure 6.5 shows the AngularJS web page in action. Note that as you type each character in the text input the model is updated, and when Enter is pressed the word is stored and the keystrokes are reset.

Listing 6.11 `directive_keyboard_events.js`: Implementing a Controller with Scope Data and Event Handlers to Support Key-Down and Key-Up Events from the View

```
01 angular.module('myApp', []).
02   controller('myController', function($scope) {
03     $scope.storedString = '';
04     $scope.keyInfo = {};
05     $scope.keyStrokes = [];
06     $scope.keyState = 'Not Pressed';
07     $scope.keyPressed = function(event){
08       if (event.keyCode == 13){
09         var element = angular.element(event.target);
10         $scope.storedString = element.val();
11         element.val('');
12         $scope.keyInfo.keyCode = event.keyCode;
13         $scope.keyStrokes = [];
14         $scope.keyState = 'Enter Pressed';
15       } else {
16         $scope.keyInfo.keyCode = event.keyCode;
17         $scope.keyStrokes.push(event.keyCode);
18         $scope.keyState = 'Not Pressed';
19       }
20     };
21   });
```

Listing 6.12 `directive_keyboard_events.html`: An AngularJS Template That Implements the `ngKeydown` and `ngKeyup` Directives

```
01 <!doctype html>
02 <html ng-app="myApp">
03 <head>
04   <title>AngularJS Keyboard Event Directives</title>
05 </head>
06 <body>
07   <div ng-controller="myController">
08     <h2>Keyboard Event Directives</h2>
09     <input type="text"
10       ng-keydown="keyState='Pressed'"
11       ng-keyup="keyPressed($event)"><hr>
12   Keyboard State:<br>
13     {{keyState}}<hr>
14   Last Key:<br>
```

```
15        {{keyInfo|json}}<hr>
16     Stored String:<br>
17        {{storedString}}<hr>
18     Recorded Key Strokes:<br>
19        {{keyStrokes}}
20     </div>
21     <script src="http://code.angularjs.org/1.3.0/angular.min.js"></script>
22     <script src="js/directive_keyboard_events.js"></script>
23 </body>
24 </html>
```

Typing keys updates model

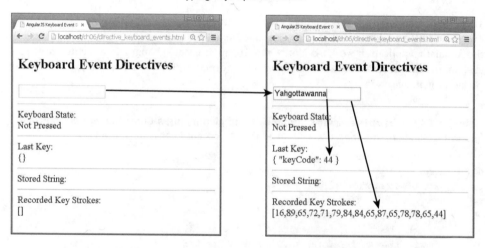

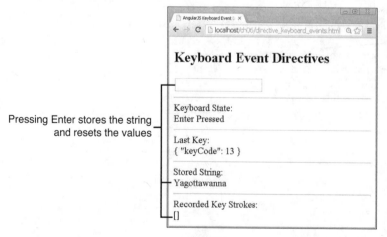

Figure 6.5   Implementing keyboard event directives in AngularJS template views.

Handling Mouse Events in the AngularJS Elements

AngularJS provides several mouse event directives that enable you to easily enhance your AngularJS applications with mouse interactivity. The most common mouse event directive that you will use is ngClick when the mouse is clicked. However, you also have several other mouse events that can come in very handy to create richly interactive components. The code in Listings 6.13 and 6.14 illustrate the usage of the ngClick, ngMouseenter, ngMouseleave, ngMousedown, ngMouseup, and ngMousemove directives.

The code in Listing 6.13 implements a controller that provides the model as well as mouseClick() and mouseMove() handler functions to handle the click and mouse movement events. The real-time mouse positioning information while the mouse is moving over the element is stored in the mouseInfo structure. Each time the mouse is clicked over the element, the click position is stored in lastClickInfo.

The code in Listing 6.14 is the AngularJS template that assigns the mouse event directives to an <img> element and displays the mouseInfo and lastClickInfo structures. Figure 6.6 shows the AngularJS application working. Notice that the mouse state changes as you enter, leave, and click on the image. Also notice that the position information is updated as you move over and click on the image.

Listing 6.13 `directive_mouse_events.js`: Implementing a Controller with Scope Data and Event Handlers to Support Mouse Click and Movement Events from the View

```
01 angular.module('myApp', []).
02   controller('myController', function($scope) {
03     $scope.mouseInfo = {};
04     $scope.lastClickInfo = {};
05     $scope.mouseClick = function(event){
06       $scope.lastClickInfo.clientX = event.clientX;
07       $scope.lastClickInfo.clientY = event.clientY;
08       $scope.lastClickInfo.screenX = event.screenX;
09       $scope.lastClickInfo.screenY = event.screenY;
10     };
11     $scope.mouseMove = function(event){
12       $scope.mouseInfo.clientX = event.clientX;
13       $scope.mouseInfo.clientY = event.clientY;
14       $scope.mouseInfo.screenX = event.screenX;
15       $scope.mouseInfo.screenY = event.screenY;
16     };
17   });
```

Listing 6.14 `directive_mouse_events.html`: An AngularJS Template That Implements the `ngClick` and Other Mouse Click and Move Event Directives

```
01 <!doctype html>
02 <html ng-app="myApp">
03 <head>
04   <title>AngularJS Event Directives</title>
05   <style>
06     img {
07       border: 3px ridge black;
08       height: 200px; width: 200px;
09       display: inline-block;
10     }
11   </style>
12 </head>
13 <body>
14   <div ng-controller="myController">
15     <h2>Event Directives</h2>
16     <img
17         src="/images/arch.jpg"
18         ng-mouseenter="mouseState='Entered'"
19         ng-mouseleave="mouseState='Left'"
20         ng-mouseclick="mouseState='Clicked'"
21         ng-mousedown="mouseState='Down'"
22         ng-mouseup="mouseState='Up'"
23         ng-click="mouseClick($event)"
24         ng-mousemove="mouseMove($event)"></img><hr/>
25    Mouse State: {{mouseState}}<br/>
26    Mouse Position Info: {{mouseInfo|json}}<br/>
27    Last Click Info: {{lastClickInfo|json}}<br/>
28   </div>
29   <script src="http://code.angularjs.org/1.3.0/angular.min.js"></script>
30   <script src="js/directive_mouse_events.js"></script>
31 </body>
32 </html>
```

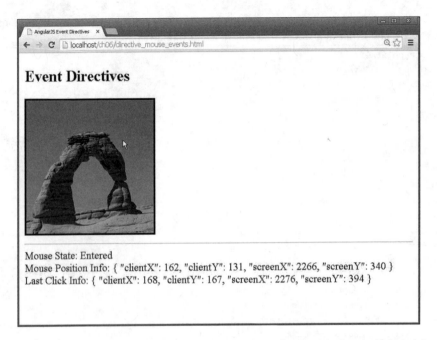

Figure 6.6   Implementing mouse-click and movement event directives in AngularJS template views.

Summary

AngularJS directives extend the behavior of HTML. You can apply directives to AngularJS templates as HTML elements, attributes, and classes. You define the functionality of directives by using JavaScript code. AngularJS provides several built-in directives that interact with form elements, bind data in the scope to the view, and interact with browser events. For example, ngModel binds the value of a form element directly to the scope. When the scope value changes, so does the value displayed by the element and vice versa.

Creating Your Own Custom Directives to Extend HTML

As with many other features of AngularJS, you can extend directive functionality by creating your own custom directives. Custom directives enable you to extend the functionality of HTML by implementing the behavior of elements yourself. If you have code that needs to manipulate the DOM, you should make this happen by using a custom directive. As with the built-in directive, custom directives provide the capability to interact with form elements, bind data in the scope to the view, and interact with browser events.

This chapter discusses the design and implementation of custom directives. You will also get a chance to see a couple of basic examples of custom directives that extend the capability of HTML.

Understanding Custom Directive Definitions

You implement custom directives by calling the `directive()` method on a `Module` object. The `directive()` method accepts the name of a directive as the first parameter and a provider function that returns an object containing the necessary instructions to build the directive object. For example, the following is a basic definition for a directive:

```
angular.module('myApp', []).
  directive('myDirective', function() {
    return {
      template: 'Name: {{name}} Score: {{score}}'
    };
  });
```

Table 7.1 provides a list of the properties you can apply to the object returned by the directive definition as `template` is returned in the preceding code.

Table 7.1   **Directive Definition Properties That Define AngularJS Directive Functionality**

Property	Description
template	Enables you to define the AngularJS template text that is inserted into the directive's element.
templateUrl	Same as template except that you specify a URL at the server, and the partial template is downloaded and inserted into the directive's element.
restrict	Enables you to specify whether the directive applies to an HTML element, an attribute, or both.
type	This is set to a string that represents the document type used by the markup. This is useful for templates that have a non-HTML root node, for example, SVG or MathML. The default value is html. ■ **html**: All root template nodes are HTML and don't need to be wrapped. Root nodes can also be top-level elements such as \<svg\> or \<math\>. ■ **svg**: The template contains only SVG content and must be wrapped in an \<svg\> node before processing. ■ **math**: The template contains only MathML content and must be wrapped in a \<math\> node before processing.
multiElement	Tells the compiler to collect DOM nodes between nodes with the attributes directive-name-start and directive-name-end, and group them together as the directive elements. You should use this option only on directives that are not strictly behavioral such as ngClick, and that do not manipulate or replace child nodes such as ngInclude.
priority	Specifies a priority number for this directive. Directives are compiled in order based on their priority starting with the directive with the highest-priority value. Prelink functions are executed in the same order starting at highest priority, but postlink function are executed in reverse starting with the lowest-priority directive.
terminal	This is a Boolean that tells the compiler to stop and not compile directives that have a lower-priority number. Any directives that have a lower-priority number than the one with terminal set to true will not be compiled.
transclude	Enables you to specify whether the directive has access to scopes outside the internal scope. This enables you to wrap the contents of an element into a new element generated when the directive is compiled and linked.
scope	Enables you to define the scope for the directive. The scope can share the parent scope, inherit from it, or have its own isolate scope.
compile	Enables you to specify a compile function that has access to the DOM element attributes. The compile function enables you to define prelink and postlink functions that can interact with and manipulate the AngularJS template DOM.

Property	Description
link	Similar to the compile function, but also provides access to the scope. The link function will be executed only if the compile function is not present. From the linking function you can register DOM event listeners as well as manipulating the DOM. The link function is executed after the template has been cloned. Typically you should put most of the template logic inside of the linking function.
controller	Enables you to define a controller within the directive to manage the directive scope and view.
controllerAs	Specifies an alias for the controller so that it can be referenced at the directive template. The directive needs to define a scope for this configuration to be used. This option is useful in the case in which the directive is used as component.
bindToController	When an isolate scope is used for a component and controllerAs is used, bindToController allows a component to have its properties bound to the controller, rather than to scope. When the controller is instantiated, the initial values of the isolate scope bindings are already available.
require	Enables you to specify other directives that are required to implement this directive. Providers for those directives must be available for an instance of this directive to be created.
template	Enables you to define the AngularJS template text that is inserted into the directive's element.

The following sections discuss the directive options in more detail.

Defining the Directive View Template

You can include AngularJS template code to build view components that will be displayed in the HTML element that contains the directive. You can add template code directly by using the template property, as in this example:

```
directive('myDirective', function() {
  return {
    template: 'Name: {{name}} Score: {{score}}'
  };
});
```

You can specify a root element in the custom template—but only one element. This element acts as the root element for any child element defined in the AngularJS template to be placed inside. Also, if you are using the transclude flag, the element should include ngTransclude. For example:

```
directive('myDirective', function() {
  return {
    transclude: true,
    template: '<div ng-transclude></div>'
  };
});
```

You can also use the `templateUrl` property to specify a URL of an AngularJS template located on the web server, as in this example:

```
directive('myDirective', function() {
  return {
    templateUrl: '/myDirective.html'
  };
});
```

The template URL can contain any standard AngularJS template code. You can therefore make your directives as simple or as complex as you need them to be.

Restricting Directive Behavior

You can apply a directive as an HTML element, an attribute, or both. The `restrict` property enables you to limit how your custom directive can be applied. The `restrict` property can be set to the following:

- **A:** Applied as an attribute name. For example:

  ```
  <my-directive></my-directive>
  ```

- **E:** Applied as an element name. For example:

  ```
  <div my-directive="expression"></div>
  ```

- **C:** Applied as a class. For example:

  ```
  <div class="my-directive: expression;"></div>
  ```

- **M:** Applied as a comment. For example:

  ```
  <!-- directive: my-directive expression -->
  ```

- **AEC:** Applied as an attribute, an element, or a class name. You can also use other combinations, such as AE or AC.

For example, you can apply the following directive as an attribute or an element:

```
directive('myDirective', function() {
  return {
    restrict: 'AE',
    templateUrl: '/myDirective.html'
  };
});
```

The following shows how to implement the directive as both an element and an attribute. Notice that the camelCase name is replaced by one with hyphens:

```
<my-directive></my-directive>
<div my-directive></div>
```

Adding a Controller to a Directive

You can add a custom controller to a directive by using the `controller` property of the directive definition. This enables you to provide controller support for the directive template. For example, the following code adds a simple controller that sets up a scope value and function:

```
directive('myDirective', function() {
  return {
    scope: {title: '='},
    controller: function ($scope){
      $scope.title = "new";
      $scope.myFunction = function(){
      });
    }
  };
});
```

You can also use the `require` option to ensure that a controller is available to the directive. The `require` option uses the `require:'^controller'` syntax to instruct the injector service to look in parent contexts until it finds the controller. The following is an example of requiring the `myController` controller in a directive:

```
directive('myDirective', function() {
  return {
    require: '^myController'
  };
});
```

When you add the `require` option, the specified controller is passed as the fourth parameter of the `link()` function. For example:

```
directive('myDirective', function() {
  return {
    require: '^myController',
    link: function(scope, element, attrs, injectedMyController){
        }
  };
});
```

You can also require multiple controllers using the `require` option in which case an array of controllers is passed to the `link()` function. For example:

```
directive('myDirective', function() {
  return {
    require: ['^myControllerA', '^myControllerB'],
    link: function(scope, element, attrs, requiredControllers){
          var controllerA = requiredControllers[0];
          var controller = requiredControllers[1];
       }
  };
});
```

If you specify the name of another directive in the `require` option, the controller for that directive is linked. For example:

```
directive('myDirective', function() {
  return {
    require: '^myOtherDirective',
    link: function(scope, element, attrs, otherDirectiveController){
       }
  };
});
```

Configuring the Directive Scope

Directives share the scope with the parent by default. This is typically adequate for most needs. The biggest downside is that you might not want to include all the custom directive properties in the parent scope, especially if the parent scope is the root scope.

To solve that problem, you can define a separate scope for the directive using the `scope` property. The following sections describe how to add an inherited scope and an isolate scope.

Adding an Inherited Scope

The simplest method to add a scope to a directive is to create one that inherits from the parent scope. The advantage is that you have a scope separate from the parent to add additional values to, but the disadvantage is that the custom directives can still modify values in the parent scope.

To create an inherited scope for the custom directive, simply set the `scope` property of the directive to `true`. For example:

```
directive('myDirective', function() {
  return {
    scope: true
  };
});
```

Adding an Isolate Scope

At times you might want to separate the scope inside a directive from the scope outside the directive. Doing so prevents the possibility of the directive changing values in the scope of the parent controller. The directive definition enables you to specify a `scope` property that creates an isolate scope. An isolate scope isolates the directive scope from the outer scope to prevent the directive from accessing the outer scope and the controller in the outer scope from altering the directive scope. For example, the following isolates the scope of the directive from the outside scope:

```
directive('myDirective', function() {
  return {
    scope: { },
    templateUrl: '/myDirective.html'
  };
});
```

Using this code, the directive has a completely empty isolate scope. However, you might want to still map some items in the outer scope to the directive's inner scope. You can use the following prefixes to attribute names to make local scope variables available in the directive's scope:

- **@:** Binds a local scope string to the value of the DOM attribute. The value of the attribute will be available inside the directive scope.

- **=:** Creates a bidirectional binding between the local `scope` property and the directive `scope` property.

- **&:** Binds a function in the local scope to the directive scope.

If no attribute name follows the prefix, the name of the directive property is used. For example,

```
title: '@'
```

is the same as

```
title: '@title'
```

The following code shows how to implement each of the methods to map local values into a directive's isolate scope:

```
angular.module('myApp', []).
  controller('myController', function($scope) {
    $scope.title="myApplication";
    $scope.myFunc = function(){
      console.log("out");
    };
  }).
  directive('myDirective', function() {
    return {
      scope: {title: '=', newFunc:"&myFunc", info: '@'},
```

```
    template: '<div ng-click="newFunc()">{{title}}: {{info}}</div>'
  };
});
```

The following code shows how to define the directive in the AngularJS template to provide the necessary attributes to map the properties:

```
<div my-directive
    my-func="myFunc()"
    title="title"
    info="SomeString"></div>
```

Transcluding Elements

Transcluding can be kind of a difficult concept to pick up on at first. Basically, the idea is that you can keep the contents of the custom directive defined in an AngularJS template and bind them to the scope. The way this works is that the linking function for the directive receives a transclusion function that is prebound to the current scope. Then elements inside the directive have access to the scope outside the directive.

You can set the `transclude` option to the following values:

- **true:** Transcludes the content of the directive.
- **'element':** Transcludes the whole element, including any directives defined at lower priorities.

You must also include the `ngTransclude` directive in elements inside your directive template. The following is an example of implementing `transclude` to access the `title` variable in the controller scope from the `myDirective` directive template:

```
angular.module('myApp', []).
  directive('myDirective', function() {
    return {
      transclude: true,
      scope: {},
      template: '<div ng-transclude>{{title}}</div>'
    };
  }).
  controller('myController', function($scope) {
    $scope.title="myApplication";
  });
```

Manipulating the DOM with a Link Function

When the AngularJS HTML compiler encounters a directive, it runs the directive's compile function, which returns the `link()` function. The `link()` function is added to the list of

AngularJS directives. After all directives have been compiled, the HTML compiler calls the `link()` functions in order, based on priority.

If you want to modify the DOM inside a custom directive, you should use a `link()` function. The `link()` function accepts the `scope`, `element`, `attributes`, `controller`, and `transclude` function associated with the directive, enabling you to manipulate the DOM directly within the directive. The transclude function is a handle that is bound to the transclusion scope.

Inside the `link()` function, you handle the `$destroy` event on the directive element and clean up anything necessary. The `link()` function is also responsible for registering DOM listeners to handle browser events.

The `link()` function uses the following syntax:

```
link: function(scope, element, attributes, [controller], [transclude])
```

The `scope` parameter is the scope of the directive, `element` is the element where the directive will be inserted, `attributes` lists the attributes declared on the element, and `controller` is the controller specified by the `require` option. The `transclude` parameter is a handle to the transclude function.

The transclude function provides access to the element created when the transclusion of the contents of the original element occurs. If you just want a transcluded element with the inherited scope, you can just call the transclude function. For example:

```
link: function link(scope, elem, attr, controller, transcludeFn){
        var transcludedElement = transcludeFn();
    }
```

You can also access the clone of the transcluded element by specifying a `clone` parameter. For example:

```
link: function link(scope, elem, attr, controller, transcludeFn){
        transcludeFn(function(clone){
          //access clone here . . .
        });
    }
```

You can also access the clone of the transcluded element with a different scope by applying a `scope` parameter as well as the `clone` parameter. For example:

```
link: function link(scope, elem, attr, controller, transcludeFn){
        transcludeFn(scope, function(clone){
          //access clone here . . .
        });
    }
```

The following directive shows the implementation of a basic `link()` function that sets a scope variable, appends data to the DOM element, implements a `$destroy` event handler, and adds a `$watch` to the scope:

```
directive('myDirective', function() {
  return {
    scope: {title: '='},
    require: '^otherDirective',
    link: function link(scope, elem, attr, controller, transclude){
      scope.title = "new";
      elem.append("Linked");
      elem.on('$destroy', function() {
        //cleanup code
      });
      scope.$watch('title', function(newVal){
        //watch code
      });
    }
  };
```

The link property can also be set to an object that includes pre and post properties that specify prelink and postlink functions. In the preceding example where link is set to a function, the function is executed as a postlink function, meaning that it is executed after the child elements are already linked, whereas the prelinked function is executed before the child elements are linked. Therefore, you should do DOM manipulation only in the postlink function. In fact, it is quite rare to need to include the prelink function.

The following shows an example of the syntax for including both the prelink and the postlink functions:

```
directive('myDirective', function() {
  return {
  link: {
    pre: function preLink(scope, elem, attr, controller){
          //prelink code
        },
    post: function postLink(scope, elem, attr, controller){
          //postlink code
        },
    }
  };
```

Manipulating the DOM with a Compile Function

The compile function is very similar to the link function with one major advantage, but several drawbacks. The advantage and really the main reason to use the compile function is performance. The compile method is executed only once when compiling the template, whereas the link function is executed each time the element is linked, for example, if you are applying multiple directives inside an ng-repeat loop or when the model changes. If you are doing a large number of DOM manipulations, that can be a big deal.

These are the limitations of the compile function:

- Any manipulations are applied before cloning takes place. That means that when the custom directive is used inside an `ng-repeat`, any DOM manipulations will be applied to *all* the custom directives generated.

- The `compile()` method cannot handle directives that recursively use themselves in their own templates or `compile()` functions because that would result in an infinite loop.

- The `compile()` method does not have access to the scope.

- The `transclude` function has been deprecated and removed from the compile function so you cannot link to the transcluded elements.

The syntax for the `compile()` method is very similar to that for the `link()` method. You can specify a single postlink function such as this:

```
directive('myDirective', function() {
  return {
  compile: function compile(scope, elem, attr, controller){
          //postlink code
          }
};
```

You can also specify pre- and postlink functions using an object as shown here:

```
directive('myDirective', function() {
  return {
  compile: {
    pre: function preLink(elem, attr){
          //prelink code
        },
    post: function postLink(elem, attr){
          //postlink code
        },
  }
};
```

Implementing Custom Directives

The types of custom directives you can define are really limitless, and this makes AngularJS really extensible. Custom directives are the most complex portion of AngularJS to explain and really to grasp. The best way to get you started is to show you some examples of custom directives, to give you a feel for how to implement them and have them interact with each other.

Manipulating the DOM in Custom Directives

One of the most common tasks you will be performing in custom directives is manipulating the DOM. This should be the only place in your AngularJS apps that you actually do manipulate the DOM. In this exercise we build a basic custom directive that applies a box with title and footer around the elements that are contained within. This example is very basic and gives you a chance to see how to use some of the mechanisms in AngularJS, such as setting values as attributes to the custom directive.

The code in Listing 7.1 creates a simple application with a controller that contains only the scope variable `title`. The code then defines a directive that enables transclusion, restricts the custom directive to element names only, and defines an isolate scope accepting the parameters `title` and `bwidth` as strings. The example also defines a `template` that adds the title bar and a `<div ng-transclude>` to store the transcluded content of the custom directive.

The `link()` function uses `append` to append a footer element. This could also have been done in the `template`; however, I wanted to illustrate that it can also be done in the `link()` function. Also note that the text of the footer element is coming from the title value of the parent scope using `scope.$parent.title`. The `link` function also adds a `border` and sets the `display` and `width` values based on the `bwidth` value in the scope.

The code in Listing 7.2 implements an AngularJS template that sets up some CSS styles and then adds the `<mybox>` custom directive that was defined in Listing 7.1. Notice that the content of the directive varies from a string to an image to a paragraph. The results are shown in Figure 7.1. Notice that the `bwidth` attribute size determines the width of the box and all the elements are surrounded by the same type of box.

Listing 7.1   `directive_custom_dom.js`: Implementing Custom Directives That Manipulate the DOM

```
01 angular.module('myApp', [])
02 .controller('myController', function($scope) {
03     $scope.title="myApplication";
04   })
05 .directive('mybox', function() {
06   return {
07     transclude: true,
08     restrict: 'E',
09     scope: {title: '@', bwidth: '@bwidth'},
10     template: '<div><span class="titleBar">{{title}}' +
11               '</span><div ng-transclude></div></div>',
12     link: function (scope, elem, attr, controller, transclude){
13         elem.append('<span class="footer">' + scope.$parent.title + '</span>');
14         elem.css('border', '2px ridge black');
```

```
15        elem.css('display', 'inline-block');
16        elem.css('width', scope.bwidth);
17      },
18    };
19  });
```

Listing 7.2 `directive_custom_dom.html`: An AngularJS Template That Utilizes a Custom Directive That Manipulates the DOM

```
01 <!doctype html>
02 <html ng-app="myApp">
03 <head>
04   <title>AngularJS Custom Directive</title>
05   <style>
06     * {text-align: center ;}
07     .titleBar { color: white; background-color: blue;
08               font: bold 14px/18px arial; display: block;}
09     .footer { color: white; background-color: blue;
10               font: italic 8px/12px arial; display: block;}
11   </style>
12 </head>
13 <body>
14   <div ng-controller="myController">
15     <h2>Custom Directive Manipulating the DOM</h2>
16     <mybox title="Simple Text" bwidth="100px">
17       Using AngularJS to build a simple box around elements.
18     </mybox>
19     <mybox title="Image" bwidth="150px">
20       <img src="/images/arch.jpg" width="150px" />
21     </mybox>
22     <mybox title="Paragraph" bwidth="200px">
23       <p>Using AngularJS to build a simple box around a paragraph.</p>
24     </mybox>
25   </div>
26   <script src="http://code.angularjs.org/1.3.0/angular.min.js"></script>
27   <script src="js/directive_custom_dom.js"></script>
28 </body>
29 </html>
```

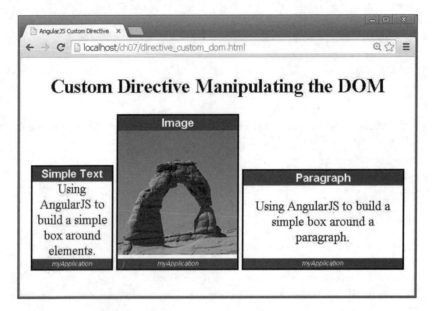

Figure 7.1   Implementing custom directives that manipulate DOM elements in AngularJS template views.

Implementing Event Handlers in a Custom Directive

Another very common use of custom directives is to implement event handlers to interact with mouse and keyboard events that are occurring in the custom elements. This enables you to provide enhanced user interactions to the custom elements.

In this example we will add mouse event handlers that enable you to use drag operations on images to resize and adjust the opacity. When the mouse is dragged left the image shrinks; right, the image enlarges; up, the image fades; and down, the opacity increases. For this example, I have included the full version of jQuery by loading it in the AngularJS template. I chose to do so to use some capabilities like getting the image width() that is not available in jQuery lite.

The code in Listing 7.3 implements two directives. The first directive is named zoomit. Notice that inside the link function, that directive listens on the mousedown, mouseup, mouseleave, and mousemove events. When the mouse button is pressed, the dragging variable is set to true, and when the mouse is released or the mouse leaves the element, dragging is set to false. Also note that in mousedown the default event behavior is suppressed by event. preventDefault(). This is to eliminate any interaction conflicts with the default browser behavior while dragging.

In the mousemove handler we determine the position movement of the mouse and increment or decrement the image size accordingly. Notice that because the full version of jQuery is loaded we were able to use the width() and height() functions to get and set the size of the image.

The fadeit directive is very similar to the zoomit directive with the exception that the opacity value of the image is changed.

The fadeit and zoomit directives are implementing in the AngularJS template shown in Listing 7.4. Notice that on the first image the zoomit directive is added, on the second image the fadeit directive is added, and on the final image both are added. This shows you that multiple custom directives can be added to the same element. The results are shown in Figure 7.2. The first image is shrunk by dragging left, the second image is faded by dragging up, and the third image is expanded and faded.

Listing 7.3 **`directive_custom_zoom.js`: Implementing Custom Directives That Register with DOM Events**

```
01 angular.module('myApp', [])
02 .directive('zoomit', function() {
03   return {
04     link: function (scope, elem, attr){
05       var dragging = false;
06       var lastX = 0;
07       elem.on('mousedown', function(event){
08         lastX = event.pageX;
09         event.preventDefault();
10         dragging = true;
11       });
12       elem.on('mouseup', function(){
13         dragging = false;
14       });
15       elem.on('mouseleave', function(){
16         dragging = false;
17       });
18       elem.on('mousemove', function(event){
19         if(dragging){
20           var adjustment = null;
21           if (event.pageX > lastX &&
22               elem.width() < 300){
23             adjustment = 1.1;
24           } else if ( elem.width() > 100){
25             adjustment = .9;
```

```
26            }
27            //requires full jQuery library
28            if(adjustment){
29              elem.width(elem.width()*adjustment);
30              elem.height(elem.height()*adjustment);
31            }
32            lastX = event.pageX;
33          }
34        });
35      }
36    };
37  })
38  .directive('fadeit', function() {
39    return {
40      link: function (scope, elem, attr){
41        var dragging = false;
42        var lastY = 0;
43        elem.on('mousedown', function(event){
44          lastY = event.pageY;
45          event.preventDefault();
46          dragging = true;
47        });
48        elem.on('mouseup', function(){
49          dragging = false;
50        });
51        elem.on('mouseleave', function(){
52          dragging = false;
53        });
54        elem.on('mousemove', function(event){
55          if(dragging){
56            var adjustment = null;
57            var currentOpacity = parseFloat(elem.css("opacity"));
58            if (event.pageY > lastY &&
59                currentOpacity < 1){
60              adjustment = 1.1;
61            } else if ( currentOpacity > 0.5){
```

```
62            adjustment = .9;
63          }
64          //requires full jQuery library
65          if(adjustment){
66            elem.css("opacity", currentOpacity*adjustment);
67          }
68          lastY = event.pageY;
69        }
70      });
71    }
72  };
73 });
```

Listing 7.4 `directive_custom_zoom.html`: An AngularJS Template That Utilizes a Custom Directive to Provide Interactions with Mouse Events

```
01 <!doctype html>
02 <html ng-app="myApp">
03 <head>
04   <title>AngularJS Custom Directive</title>
05   <style>
06     img { width: 200px; }
07   </style>
08 </head>
09 <body>
10   <h2>Custom Directive Zoom and Fade</h2>
11   <img src="/images/pyramid.jpg" zoomit></img>
12   <img src="/images/pyramid.jpg" fadeit></img>
13   <img src="/images/pyramid.jpg" zoomit fadeit></img>
14   <script
➥src="http://ajax.googleapis.com/ajax/libs/jquery/1.11.1/jquery.min.js"></script>
15   <script src="http://code.angularjs.org/1.3.0/angular.min.js"></script>
16   <script src="js/directive_custom_zoom.js"></script>
17 </body>
18 </html>
```

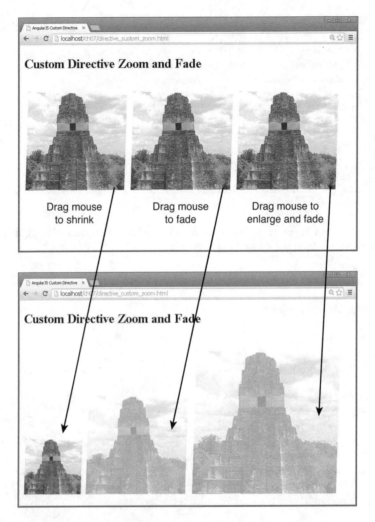

Figure 7.2   Implementing custom directives that provide interactions with mouse events to manipulate DOM elements.

Implementing Nested Directives

The final example illustrates how you can nest directives within each other and have them interact. Nesting directives is a great way to provide a parent context and container for custom elements that are related to each other. In this example the outer directive myPhotos acts as a container that can contain child directives named myPhoto.

Listing 7.5 implements two custom directives: myPhotos and myPhoto. The myPhotos directive is designed to be a container for the myPhoto directive. Notice that lines 7–18 define a controller that provides the functionality for the myPhotos directive, including an addPhoto() function. Because the code uses require:'^myPhotos' in the myPhoto directive, you can also call the addPhoto() method from the link() function by using the photosControl handle to the myPhotos controller.

Listing 7.6 implements the myPhotos and myPhoto directives in an AngularJS template. The myPhoto directives are nested inside the myPhotos directive. Notice that the title attribute is set on each myPhoto directive and linked to the scope in line 28 of Listing 7.5.

Listing 7.7 implements a partial template loaded by the myPhotos directive. It generates a <div> container and then uses the photos array in the myPhotos scope to build a list of links bound to the select() function, using ng-click. <div ng-transclude></div> provides the container for the myPhoto child elements.

Figure 7.3 shows the web page created by Listings 7.5, 7.6, and 7.7.

Listing 7.5 `directive_custom_photos.js`: Implementing Custom Directives That Interact with Each Other

```
01 angular.module('myApp', [])
02 .directive('myPhotos', function() {
03   return {
04     restrict: 'E',
05     transclude: true,
06     scope: {},
07     controller: function($scope) {
08       var photos = $scope.photos = [];
09       $scope.select = function(photo) {
10         angular.forEach(photos, function(photo) {
11           photo.selected = false;
12         });
13         photo.selected = true;
14       };
15       this.addPhoto = function(photo) {
16         photos.push(photo);
17       };
18     },
19     templateUrl: 'my_photos.html'
20   };
21 })
22 .directive('myPhoto', function() {
23   return {
24     require: '^myPhotos',
25     restrict: 'E',
26     transclude: true,
```

```
27    scope: { title: '@'},
28    link: function(scope, elem, attrs, photosControl) {
29      photosControl.addPhoto(scope);
30    },
31    template: '<div ng-show="selected" ng-transclude></div>'
32  };
33 });
```

Listing 7.6   `directive_custom.html`: An AngularJS Template That Implements Nested Custom Directives

```
01 <!doctype html>
02 <html ng-app="myApp">
03 <head>
04   <title>AngularJS Custom Directive</title>
05   <style>
06     img { width: 300px }
07   </style>
08 </head>
09 <body>
10   <h2>Custom Directive Photo Flip</h2>
11     <my-photos>
12       <my-photo title="Flower">
13         <img src="/images/flower.jpg"/>
14       </my-photo>
15       <my-photo title="Arch">
16         <img src="/images/arch.jpg"/>
17       </my-photo>
18       <my-photo title="Lake">
19         <img src="/images/lake.jpg"/>
20       </my-photo>
21       <my-photo title="Bison">
22         <img src="/images/bison.jpg"/>
23       </my-photo>
24     </my-photos>
25   <script src="http://code.angularjs.org/1.3.0/angular.min.js"></script>
26   <script src="js/directive_custom_photos.js"></script>
27 </body>
28 </html>
```

Listing 7.7 `my_photos.html`: A Partial AngularJS Template That Provides the Root Element for the `myPhotos` Custom Directive

```
01 <div>
02   <span ng-repeat="photo in photos"
03         ng-class="{active:photo.selected}">
04     <a href="" ng-click="select(photo)">{{photo.title}}</a>
05   </span>
06   <div ng-transclude></div>
07 </div>
```

Figure 7.3   Implementing event directives in AngularJS template views.

Summary

One of the most powerful features of AngularJS is the capability to create your own custom directives. Implementing a custom directive in code is simple using the `directive()` method on a `Module` object. However, directives can also be very complex because of the myriad ways they can be implemented. This chapter has given you a small taste of what can be done with custom directives in AngularJS. I would recommend spending some time playing around with the examples and writing some of your own to familiarize yourself as much as possible with how they work.

Using Events to Interact with Data in the Model

Events are one of the most critical components in most AngularJS applications. Events enable users to interact with elements as well as the application to know when to perform certain tasks. This chapter discusses different types of events that you have and will be working within your AngularJS applications to provide a perspective and introduce you to some new topics.

Specifically, this chapter discusses four types of events, including browser events, user interaction events, scope-based events, and custom events. You have already been introduced to some of this in previous chapters. The reason this is positioned here is that the previous chapters give perspective to the discussion here.

Browser Events

There are several events that are triggered by the browser itself. In a way these are also user-interaction events; however, I want to keep them separate for this discussion. The browser events include things like the ready event when the document is loaded, as well as the resize event when the browser is resized.

These are useful to know when the view of the user is changing. You have already seen how to use the .on() function to add handlers for events; the question is where to put the handler. The best solutions I've seen involve a handler that is registered in the run block for the entire application. Any information can then be made available to subsequent components through the scope model or through a cache service.

User Interaction Events

You have already been exposed to user interaction events. These include mouse and keyboard events, as well as other events such as the focus and blur events. There are typically two places where you will implement interactions for user events. One is using the ng event directives, such as ng-click, and simple interactions in the view and controller code. The second place to add user event interactions is in the link function of custom directives.

You have already been exposed to both of these methods in previous chapters; what I wanted to point out here is that you do have a choice of which one you want to use. The advantage of using the built-in ng event directives such as ngClick is that you do not have to add the complexity of creating a custom directive for simple requirements.

There are a couple of downsides to using the ng event directives, though. One is that you should not be doing DOM manipulation in the controller, which is where you can define handlers for the ng directives. Another downside is that you will have to implement the ngClick code in the template every time you want the functionality. For example, consider the following template code to add mouse event handlers to an element:

```
<span
  ng-mouseenter="mouseEntered(event)"
  ng-mouseleave="mouseLeft(event)"
  ng-click="clicked(event)">
<span>
```

The code isn't too bad, but what if there are several different locations where you want the same functionality? If they fall in an ng-repeat block, it's not too bad, but otherwise it's a pain. A good rule to follow is that if you want to use the functionality in more than one place and definitely if you will reuse it in multiple applications, you should define a custom directive that implements the handlers.

Adding $watches to Track Scope Change Events

Another common event that you will be using is triggered not by the browser, but by changes to the data in the model. This capability enables you to react to model changes without having to add code at every point where the values might change. This capability is useful because often the data in the model might be changing in various ways—user input, service updates, and so on.

Using $watch to Track a Scope Variable

To add the capability to handle changes to scope values, you simply need to add a $watch to the variable in the scope using the $watch functionality built into AngularJS. The $watch function in the scope uses the following syntax:

```
$watch(watchExpression, listener, [objectEquality])
```

The *watchExpression* is the expression in the scope to watch. This expression is called on every $digest() and will return the value that will be watched. The listener defines a function that will be called when the value of the *watchExpression* changes to a new value. The *listener* will not be called if the *watchExpression* is changed to the value it is already set to.

The *objectEquality* is a Boolean that when true will use the `angular.equals()` function to determine equality instead of the more strict `==!` operator. You should be careful when using *objectEquality* because on complex objects it can result in increases in memory and performance usage.

The following shows an example of adding `$watch` on the scope variable score:

```
$scope.score = 0;
$scope.$watch('score', function(newValue, oldValue) {
  if(newValue > 10){
    $scope.status = 'win';
  }
});
```

Using `$watchGroup` to Track Multiple Scope Variables

AngularJS also provides the capability to watch an array of expressions using the `$watchGroup` method. The `$watchGroup` method works the same as `$watch` except that the first parameter is an array of expressions to watch. The listener will be passed an array with the new and old values for the watched variables. For example, if you wanted to watch the variables `score` and `time`, you would use this:

```
$scope.score = 0;
$scope.time = 0;
$scope.$watchGroup(['score', 'time'], function(newValues, oldValues) {
  if(newValues[0] > 10){
    $scope.status = 'win';
  } else if (newValues[1] > 5{
    $scope.status = 'times up';
});
```

Using `$watchCollection` to Track Changes to Properties of an Object in the Scope

You can also watch the properties of an object using the `$watchCollection` method. The `$watchCollection` method takes an object as the first parameter and watches the properties of the object. In the case of an array, the individual values of the array are watched. For example:

```
$scope.scores = [5, 10, 15, 20];
$scope.$watchGroup('scores', function(newValue, oldValue) {
  $scope.newScores = newValue;
});
```

Implementing Watches in a Controller

The code in Listings 8.1 and 8.2 demonstrate a simple example that implements the $watch, $watchGroup, and $watchCollection methods. The code in Listing 8.1 implements a controller that stores the values myColor, hits, and misses, as well as an object named myObj, in the scope. There are event handlers that update those values based on mouse clicks. Then in lines 18–25 the $watch, $watchGroup, and $watchCollection methods are implemented that adjust the object and a changes variable as the values change.

The code in Listing 8.2 implements an AngularJS template that enables the user to use the mouse to select the color and increment the hits and misses variables. The object and change values are displayed at the bottom, showing how the $watch methods detect and update changes to the scope. Figure 8.1 shows the rendered AngularJS web page.

Listing 8.1   **scope_watch.js: Implementing $watch(), $watchGroup() and $watchCollection() Handlers to Watch the Value of Scope Variables**

```
01 angular.module('myApp', [])
02 .controller('myController', function ($scope) {
03   $scope.mColors = ['red', 'green', 'blue'];
04   $scope.myColor = '';
05   $scope.hits = 0;
06   $scope.misses = 0;
07   $scope.changes = 0;
08   $scope.myObj = {color: '', hits: '', misses: ''};
09   $scope.setColor = function (color){
10     $scope.myColor = color;
11   };
12   $scope.hit = function (){
13     $scope.hits += 1;
14   };
15   $scope.miss = function (){
16     $scope.misses += 1;
17   };
18   $scope.$watch('myColor', function (newValue, oldValue){
19     $scope.myObj.color = newValue;
20   });
21   $scope.$watchGroup(['hits', 'misses'], function (newValue, oldValue){
22     $scope.myObj.hits = newValue[0];
23     $scope.myObj.misses = newValue[1];
24   });
25   $scope.$watchCollection('myObj', function (newValue, oldValue){
26     $scope.changes += 1;
27   });
28 });
```

Listing 8.2   **scope_watch.html**: HTML Template Code That Provides the View and
Interactions with the Scope and Controller Defined in Listing 8.1

```
01 <!doctype html>
02 <html ng-app="myApp">
03   <head>
04     <title>AngularJS Scope Variable Watch</title>
05     <style>
06     </style>
07   </head>
08   <body>
09     <h2>Watching Values in the AngularJS Scope</h2>
10     <div ng-controller="myController">
11       Select Color:
12       <span ng-repeat="mColor in mColors">
13         <span ng-style="{color: mColor}"
14               ng-click="setColor(mColor)">
15         {{mColor}}</span>
16       </span><hr>
17       <span ng-click="hit()">[+]</span>
18       Hits: {{hits}}<br>
19       <span ng-click="miss()">[+]</span>
20       misses: {{misses}}<hr>
21       Object: {{myObj|json}} <br>
22       Number of Changes: {{changes}}
23     </div>
24     <script src="http://code.angularjs.org/1.3.0/angular.min.js"></script>
25     <script src="js/scope_watch.js"></script>
26   </body>
27 </html>
```

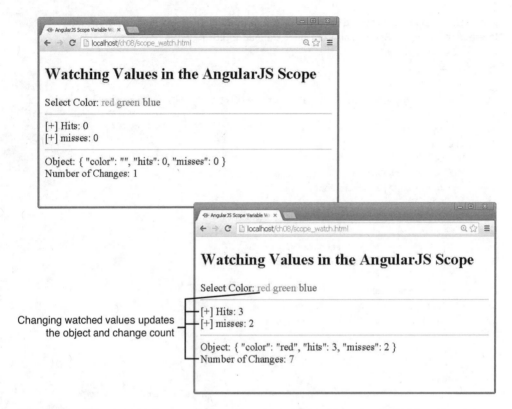

Figure 8.1   Using `$watch()`, `$watchGroup()`, and `$watchCollection()` handlers to watch the value of scope variables.

Emitting and Broadcasting Custom Events

A great feature of scopes is the capability to emit and broadcast events within the scope hierarchy. Events enable you to send notification to different levels in the scope that an event has occurred. Events can be anything you choose, such as a value changed or threshold reached. This is extremely useful in many situations, such as letting child scopes know that a value has changed in a parent scope or vice versa.

Emitting a Custom Event to the Parent Scope Hierarchy

To emit an event from a scope, you use the `$emit()` method. This method sends an event upward through the parent scope hierarchy. Any ancestor scopes that have registered for the event are notified. The `$emit()` method uses the following syntax, where *name* is the event name and *args* is zero or more arguments to pass to the event handler functions:

```
scope.$emit(name, [args, . . .])
```

Broadcasting a Custom Event to the Child Scope Hierarchy

You can also broadcast an event downward through the child scope hierarchy by using the `$broadcast()` method. Any descendent scopes that have registered for the event are notified. The `$broadcast()` method uses the following syntax, where *name* is the event name and *args* is zero or more arguments to pass to the event handler functions:

```
scope.$broadcast(name, [args, . . .])
```

Handling Custom Events with a Listener

To handle an event that is emitted or broadcasted, you use the `$on()` method. The `$on()` method uses the following syntax, where *name* is the name of the event to listen for:

```
scope.$on(name, listener)
```

The *listener* parameter is a function that accepts the event as the first parameter and any arguments passed by the `$emit()` or `$broadcast()` method as subsequent parameters. The event object has the following properties:

- **targetScope:** The scope from which `$emit()` or `$broadcast()` was called.
- **currentScope:** The scope that is currently handling the event.
- **name:** The name of the event.
- **stopPropagation():** A function that stops the event from being propagated up or down the scope hierarchy.
- **preventDefault():** A function that prevents default behavior in a browser event but only executes your own custom code.
- **defaultPrevented:** A Boolean that is `true` if `event.preventDefault()` has been called.

Implementing Custom Events in Nested Controllers

Listings 8.3 and 8.4 illustrate the use of `$emit()`, `$broadcast()`, and `$on()` to send and handle events up and down the scope hierarchy. In Listing 8.3, lines 2–15 implement a parent scope controller called `Characters`, and lines 16–32 define a child scope controller named `Character`.

Also in Listing 8.3, the `changeName()` function changes the `currentName` value and then broadcasts a `CharacterChanged` event. The `CharacterChanged` event is handled in lines

26–28, using the `$on()` method, and sets the `currentInfo` value in the scope, which will update the page elements.

Notice that line 6 of Listing 8.3 uses the `this` keyword to access the `name` property. The `name` property actually comes from a dynamic child scope that was created because the following directives were used to generate multiple elements in Listing 8.4. The child scope can be accessed from the `changeName()` method in the scope by using the `this` keyword:

```
ng-repeat="name in names"
ng-click="changeName()"
```

Lines 9–14 of Listing 8.3 implement a handler for the `CharacterDeleted` event that removes the character `name` from the `names` property. The child controller in line 27 broadcasts this event via `$broadcast()`.

The AngularJS template code in Listing 8.4 implements the nested `ng-controller` statements, which generates the scope hierarchy and displays scope values for the characters. This code also includes some very basic CSS styling to make spans look like buttons and to position elements on the page. Figure 8.2 shows the resulting web page. As you click a character name, information about that character is displayed, and when you click the Delete button, the character is deleted from the buttons and the Info section.

Listing 8.3 `scope_events.js`: Implementing `$emit()` and `$broadcast()` Events within the Scope Hierarchy

```
01 angular.module('myApp', []).
02   controller('Characters', function($scope) {
03     $scope.names = ['Frodo', 'Aragorn', 'Legolas', 'Gimli'];
04     $scope.currentName = $scope.names[0];
05     $scope.changeName = function() {
06       $scope.currentName = this.name;
07       $scope.$broadcast('CharacterChanged', this.name);
08     };
09     $scope.$on('CharacterDeleted', function(event, removeName){
10       var i = $scope.names.indexOf(removeName);
11       $scope.names.splice(i, 1);
12       $scope.currentName = $scope.names[0];
13       $scope.$broadcast('CharacterChanged', $scope.currentName);
14     });
15   }).
16   controller('Character', function($scope) {
17     $scope.info = {'Frodo': { weapon: 'Sting',
18                               race: 'Hobbit'},
19                   'Aragorn': { weapon: 'Sword',
20                               race: 'Man'},
21                   'Legolas': { weapon: 'Bow',
22                               race: 'Elf'},
23                   'Gimli': { weapon: 'Axe',
```

```
24                        race: 'Dwarf'}};
25      $scope.currentInfo = $scope.info['Frodo'];
26      $scope.$on('CharacterChanged', function(event, newCharacter){
27        $scope.currentInfo = $scope.info[newCharacter];
28      });
29      $scope.deleteChar = function() {
30        delete $scope.info[$scope.currentName];
31        $scope.$emit('CharacterDeleted', $scope.currentName);
32      };
33    });
```

Listing 8.4   **scope_events.html**: HTML Template Code That Renders the Scope Hierarchy for Listing 8.3 Controllers

```
01  <!doctype html>
02  <html ng-app="myApp">
03    <head>
04      <title>AngularJS Scope Events</title>
05      <style>
06        span{
07          padding: 3px; border: 3px ridge;
08          cursor: pointer; width: 100px; display: inline-block;
09          font: bold 18px/22px Georgia; text-align: center;
10          color: white; background-color: blue }
11        label{
12          padding: 2px; margin: 5px 10px; font: 15px bold;
13          display: inline-block; width: 50px; text-align: right; }
14        .lList {
15          vertical-align: top;
16          display: inline-block; width: 130px; }
17        .cInfo {
18          display: inline-block; width: 175px;
19          border: 3px blue ridge; padding: 3px; }
20      </style>
21    </head>
22    <body>
23      <h2>Custom Events in Nested Controllers</h2>
24      <div ng-controller="Characters">
25        <div class="lList">
26            <span ng-repeat="name in names"
27                  ng-click="changeName()">{{name}}
28            </span>
29        </div>
30        <div class="cInfo">
31            <div ng-controller="Character">
32              <label>Name: </label>{{currentName}}<br>
```

```
33              <label>Race: </label>{{currentInfo.race}}<br>
34              <label>Weapon: </label>{{currentInfo.weapon}}<br>
35              <span ng-click="deleteChar()">Delete</span>
36          </div>
37        </div>
38      </div>
39      <script src="http://code.angularjs.org/1.3.0/angular.min.js"></script>
40      <script src="js/scope_events.js"></script>
41    </body>
42  </html>
```

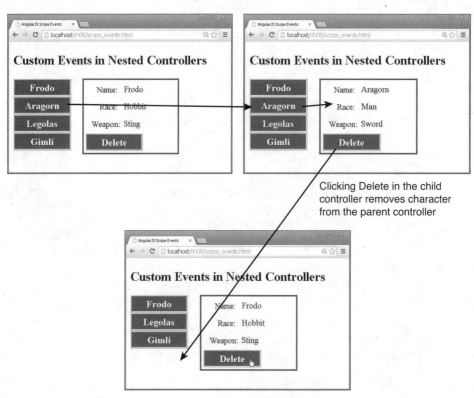

Figure 8.2   Using $broadcast() and $emit() to send change and delete events through a scope hierarchy.

Summary

The capability to manage events is one of the most critical components in most AngularJS applications. You can use events in AngularJS applications to provide user interaction with elements as well as components of the application communicating with each other to know when to perform certain tasks. This chapter started off with a brief discussion about browser and user interaction events and how they relate to the overall application architecture.

Next the chapter covered using the `$watch`, `$watchGroup`, and `$watchCollection` methods to watch values in the scope. Using watches allows you to act on changes to the scope values without having to place code in every location where those values might change.

Scopes are organized into hierarchies, and the root scope is defined at that application level. Each instance of a controller also gets an instance of a child scope. In this chapter you learned how to emit or broadcast events from within a scope and then implement handlers that listen for those events and get executed when they are triggered.

Implementing AngularJS Services in Web Applications

One of the most fundamental components of AngularJS functionality is services. Services provide task-based functionality to your applications. Think about a service as a chunk of reusable code that performs one or more related tasks. AngularJS provides several built-in services and also enables you to create your own customized services.

This chapter introduces the AngularJS services. You will get a chance to see and implement some of the built-in services, such as `$http` for web server communication, `$cookieStore` for storing and retrieving browser cookies, and `$animate` to provide animation capabilities.

Understanding AngularJS Services

AngularJS services are singleton objects, which means only one instance is ever created. The intent of a service is to provide a concise bit of code that performs specific tasks. A service can be as simple as providing a value definition or as complex as providing full HTTP communication to a web server.

A service provides a container for reusable functionality that is readily available to AngularJS applications. Services are defined and registered with the dependency injection mechanism in AngularJS. This enables you to inject services into modules, controllers, and other services.

> **Note**
>
> Chapter 3, "Understanding AngularJS Application Dynamics," discusses dependency injection. You should read that chapter, if you haven't already, before continuing with this one.

Using the Built-in Services

AngularJS provides several built-in services. These are automatically registered with the dependency injector, and you can therefore easily incorporate them into your AngularJS applications by using dependency injection.

Table 9.1 describes some of the most common built-in services to give you an idea of what is available. The following sections cover some of these services in more detail.

Table 9.1 **Common Services That Are Built In to AngularJS**

Service	Description
`$anchorScroll`	Provides the capability to scroll to a page anchor specified in `$location.hash()` based on the rules defined in the HTML5 spec.
`$animate`	Provides animation hooks to link into both CSS- and JavaScript-based animations.
`$cacheFactory`	Provides the capability to put key/value pairs into an object cache, where they can be retrieved later by other code components using the same service.
`$compile`	Provides the capability to compile an HTML string or a DOM object into a template and produce a template function that can link the scope and template together.
`$cookies`	Provides read and write access to the browser's cookies.
`$document`	Specifies a jQuery-wrapped reference to the browser's `window.document` element.
`$exceptionHandler`	Specifies a handler to which uncaught exceptions in AngularJS expressions are delegated.
`$http`	Provides a simple-to-use functionality to send HTTP requests to the web server or another service.
`$ingerpolate`	Compiles a string with markup into an interpolation function.
`$interval`	Provides access to a browser's `window.setInterval` functionality.
`$locale`	Provides localization rules that are consumed by various AngularJS components.
`$location`	Provides the capability to interact with a browser's `window.location` object.
`$log`	Provides a simple logging service.
`$parse`	Parses an AngularJS expression string into a JavaScript function.
`$q`	Provides a promise/deferred implementation service.

Service	Description
$resource	Enables you to create an object that can interact with a RESTful server-side data source.
$rootElement	Provides access to the root element in the AngularJS application.
$rootScope	Provides access to the root scope for the AngularJS application.
$route	Provides deep-linking URL support for controllers and views by watching the $location.url() and mapping the path to existing route definitions.
$routeParams	Provides a service that enables you to retrieve the current set of parameters in the route.
$sanitize	Provides a service that can be used to sanitize input by parsing the HTML into tokens.
$sce	Provides strict contextual escaping functionality when handling data from untrusted sources.
$swipe	Provides a service that makes implementing device swipe types of directives easier.
$templateCache	Provides the capability to read templates from a web server into a cache for later use.
$timeout	Provides access to a browser's window.setTimeout functionality.
$window	Specifies a jQuery-wrapped reference to the browser's window element.

Sending HTTP GET and PUT Requests with the $http Service

The $http service enables you to directly interact with the web server from your AngularJS code. The $http service uses the browser's XMLHttpRequest object underneath, but from the context of the AngularJS framework.

There are two ways to use the $http service. The simplest is to use one of the following built-in shortcut methods that correspond to standard HTTP requests:

- delete(url, [config])
- get(url, [config])
- head(url, [config])
- jsonp(url, [config])
- post(url, data, [config])
- put(url, data, [config])
- patch(url, data, [config])

Configuring the `$http` Request

In these methods, the `url` parameter is the URL of the web request. The optional `config` parameter is a JavaScript object that specifies the options to use when implementing the request. Table 9.2 lists the properties you can set in the `config` parameter.

You can also specify the request, URL, and data by sending the `config` parameter directly to the `$http(config)` method. For example, the following two lines are exactly the same:

```
$http.get('/myUrl');
$http({method: 'GET', url:'/myUrl'});
```

Table 9.2　**Properties That Can Be Defined in the `config` Parameter for `$http` Service Requests**

Property	Description
method	An HTTP method, such as GET or POST.
url	The URL of the resource that is being requested.
params	Parameters to be sent. This can be a string in the format `?key1=value1&key2=value2&...` or it can be an object, in which case it is turned into a JSON string.
data	Data to be sent as the request message data. By default data is posted to the server as JSON.
headers	Headers to send with the request. You can specify an object containing the header names to be sent as properties. If a property in the object has a null value, the header is not sent.
xsrfHeaderName	The name of the HTTP header to populate with the XSRF token.
xsrfCookieName	The name of the cookie containing the XSRF token.
transformRequest	A function that is called to transform/serialize the request headers and body. The function accepts the body data as the first parameter and a getter function to get the headers by name as the second. For example: `function(data, getHeader)`
transformResponse	A function that is called to transform/deserialize the response headers and body. The function accepts the body data as the first parameter and a getter function to get the headers by name as the second. For example: `function(data, getHeader)`
cache	A Boolean that, when `true`, indicates that a default `$http` cache is used to cache GET responses; otherwise, if a cache instance is built with `$cacheFactory`, that cache is used for caching. If `false` and there is no `$cacheFactory` built, the responses are not cached.
timeout	The timeout, in milliseconds, when the request should be aborted.

Property	Description
withCredentials	A Boolean that, when true, indicates that the withCredentials flag on the XHR object is set.
responseType	The type of response to expect, such as json or text.

Implementing the $http Response Callback Functions

When you call a request method by using the $http object, you get back an object with the promise methods success() and error(). You can pass to these methods a callback function that is called if the request is successful or if it fails. These methods accept the following parameters:

- **data:** Response data.

- **status:** Response status.

- **header:** Response header.

- **config:** Request configuration.

The following is a simple example of implementing the success() and error() methods on a get() request:

```
$http({method: 'GET', url: '/myUrl'}).
  success(function(data, status, headers, config) {
    // handle success
  }).
  error(function(data, status, headers, config) {
    // handle failure
  });
```

Implementing a Simple HTTP Server and Using the $http Service to Access It

The code in Listings 9.1 through 9.3 implements a simple Node.js web service and AngularJS application that accesses it. The web server contains a simple JavaScript object with items and count to mimic the stock of a store. The web application enables a user to tell the server to restock the store, and buy and use items. The example is very rudimentary so that the code is easy to follow, but it incorporates GET and POST requests as well as error-handling examples.

Listing 9.1 implements the Node.js web server that handles the GET route /reset/data and the POST route /buy/item. If the count of an item is zero, the /buy/item route returns an HTTP error. The first few lines simply set up the Node.js server. Don't worry if you don't follow exactly what is happening there. The initStore() function initializes the products and counts for items. On line 17 the GET route /reset/data is initialized and returns the store object as JSON. On line 21 the POST rout is initialized. This route decrements the item count and returns the store data (typically it would not need to return the full data, but for this simple example it makes the code cleaner). If the item is out of stock, a 400 error is returned.

> **Note**
>
> You will need to stop the normal `server.js` HTTP server if it is running before starting
> `service_server.js` from Listing 9.1. Also, you will want to place the `service_server.js`
> file from Listing 9.1 in the parent folder to the `service_http.html` in Listing 9.2 for the paths
> to match up properly in the Node.js static routes. The structure should look similar
> to this:
>
> ```
> ./service_server.js
> ./ch09/service_http.html
> ./ch09/js/service_http.js
> ```

Listing 9.1 `service_server.js`: Implementing an Express Server That Supports GET and POST Routes for an AngularJS Controller

```
01 var express = require('express');
02 var bodyParser = require('body-parser');
03 var app = express();
04 app.use('/', express.static('./'));
05 app.use(bodyParser.urlencoded({ extended: true }));
06 app.use(bodyParser.json());
07 function initStore(){
08   var items = ['eggs', 'toast', 'bacon', 'juice'];
09   var storeObj = {};
10   for (var itemIDX in items){
11     storeObj[items[itemIDX]] =
12       Math.floor(Math.random() * 5 + 1);
13   }
14   return storeObj;
15 }
16 var storeItems = initStore();
17 app.get('/reset/data', function(req, res){
18   storeItems = initStore();
19   res.json(storeItems);
20 });
21 app.post('/buy/item', function(req, res){
22   if (storeItems[req.body.item] > 0){
23     storeItems[req.body.item] =
24       storeItems[req.body.item] - 1;
25     res.json(storeItems);
26   }else {
27     res.json(400, { msg: 'Sorry ' + req.body.item +
28                     ' is out of stock.' });
29   }
30 });
31 app.listen(80);
```

Listing 9.2 implements the AngularJS application and controller. Notice that the `buyItem()` method calls the `/buy/item` POST route on the server and places the results in the scope variable `$scope.storeItems`. If an error occurs, the `$scope.status` variable is set to the `msg` value in the error response object. The `resetStore()` method calls the `/reset/data` GET route on the server and updates `$scope.storeItems` with the successful response.

Listing 9.3 implements an AngularJS template that includes the Restock Store button, status message on error, and a list of store items. Figure 9.1 shows how the item counts get adjusted when items are bought and used, and the out-of-stock error message is shown when the user tries to buy an out-of-stock item.

Listing 9.2 `service_http.js`: Implementing an AngularJS Controller That Interacts with the Web Server Using the `$http` Service

```
01 angular.module('myApp', []).
02   controller('myController', ['$scope', '$http',
03                               function($scope, $http) {
04     $scope.storeItems = {};
05     $scope.kitchenItems = {};
06     $scope.status = "";
07     $scope.resetStore = function(){
08       $scope.status = "";
09       $http.get('/reset/data')
10           .success(function(data, status, headers, config) {
11               $scope.storeItems = data;
12           })
13           .error(function(data, status, headers, config) {
14               $scope.status = data;
15           });
16     };
17     $scope.buyItem = function(buyItem){
18       $http.post('/buy/item', {item:buyItem})
19           .success(function(data, status, headers, config) {
20               $scope.storeItems = data;
21               if($scope.kitchenItems.hasOwnProperty(buyItem)){
22                 $scope.kitchenItems[buyItem] += 1;
23               } else {
24                 $scope.kitchenItems[buyItem] = 1;
25               }
26               $scope.status = "Purchased " + buyItem;
27           })
28           .error(function(data, status, headers, config) {
29               $scope.status = data.msg;
30           });
31     };
32     $scope.useItem = function(useItem){
33       if($scope.kitchenItems[useItem] > 0){
```

```
34           $scope.kitchenItems[useItem] -= 1;
35       }
36     };
37   }]);
```

Listing 9.3 `service_http.html`: An AngularJS Template That Implements Directives That Are Linked to Web Server Data

```
01 <!doctype html>
02 <html ng-app="myApp">
03 <head>
04   <title>AngularJS $http Service</title>
05   <style>
06     span {
07       color:red; cursor: pointer; }
08     .myList {
09       display: inline-block; width: 200px;
10       vertical-align: top; }
11   </style>
12 </head>
13 <body>
14   <div ng-controller="myController">
15     <h2>GET and POST Using $http Service</h2>
16     <input type="button" ng-click="resetStore()"
17            value="Restock Store"/>
18     {{status}}
19     <hr>
20     <div class="myList">
21         <h3>The Store</h3>
22         <div ng-repeat="(item, count) in storeItems">
23           {{item}} ({{count}})
24           [<span ng-click="buyItem(item)">buy</span>]
25         </div>
26     </div>
27     <div class="myList">
28       <h3>My Kitchen</h3>
29       <div ng-repeat="(item, count) in kitchenItems">
30         {{item}} ({{count}})
31         [<span ng-click="useItem(item)">use</span>]
32       </div>
33     </div>
34   </div>
35   <script src="http://code.angularjs.org/1.3.0/angular.min.js"></script>
36   <script src="js/service_http.js"></script>
37 </body>
38 </html>
```

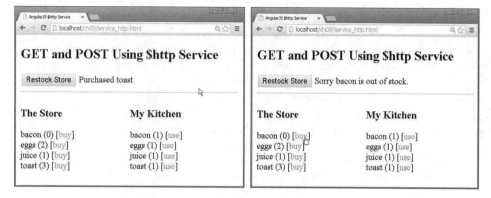

Figure 9.1   Implementing the $http service to allow AngularJS controllers to interact with the web server.

Using the $cacheFactory Service

The $cacheFactory service provides a very handy repository for temporarily storing data as key/value pairs. Because $cacheFactory is a service, it is available to multiple controllers and other AngularJS components.

When creating the $cacheFactory service, you can specify an options object that contains the capacity property—for example, {capacity: 5}. By adding this capacity setting, you limit the maximum number of elements in the cache to five. When a new item is added, the oldest item is removed. If no capacity is specified, the cache continues to grow.

Listing 9.4 illustrates a basic example of implementing $cacheFactory in a Module object and then accessing it from two different controllers.

Listing 9.4   `service_cache.js`: Implementing a $cacheFactory Service in an AngularJS Application

```
01 var app = angular.module('myApp', []);
02 app.factory('MyCache', function($cacheFactory) {
03   return $cacheFactory('myCache', {capacity:5});
04 });
05 app.controller('myController', ['$scope', 'MyCache',
06                                 function($scope, cache) {
07     cache.put('myValue', 55);
08   }]);
09 app.controller('myController2', ['$scope', 'MyCache',
10                                 function($scope, cache) {
11   $scope.value = cache.get('myValue');
12 }]);
```

Implementing Browser Alerts Using the `$window` Service

The `$window` service provides a jQuery wrapper for a browser's `window` object, allowing you to access the `window` object as you normally would from JavaScript. To illustrate this, the following code pops up a browser alert, using the `alert()` method on the `window` object. The message of the alert gets data from the `$window.screen.availWidth` and `$window.screen.availHeight` properties of the browser's `window` object:

```
var app = angular.module('myApp', []);
app.controller('myController', ['$scope', '$window',
                                function($scope, window) {
    window.alert("Your Screen is: \n" +
        window.screen.availWidth + "X" + window.screen.availHeight);
}]);
```

Interacting with Browser Cookies Using the `$cookieStore` Service

AngularJS provides a couple of services for getting and setting cookies: `$cookie` and `$cookieStore`. Cookies provide temporary storage in a browser and persist even when the user leaves the web page or closes the browser.

The `$cookie` service enables you to get and change string cookie values by using dot notation. For example, the following code retrieves the value of a cookie with the name `appCookie` and then changes it:

```
var cookie = $cookies.appCookie;
$cookies.appCookie = 'New Value';
```

The `$cookieStore` service provides `get()`, `put()`, and `remove()` functions to get, set, and remove cookies. A nice feature of the `$cookieStore` service is that it serializes JavaScript object values to a JSON string before setting them, and then it deserializes them back to objects when getting them.

To use the `$cookie` and `$cookieStore` services, you need to do three things. First, you load the `angular-cookies.js` library in the template after `angular.js` but before `application.js`. For example:

```
<script src="http://code.angularjs.org/1.3.0/angular.min.js"></script>
<script src="http://code.angularjs.org/1.3.0/angular-cookies.min.js"></script>
```

> **Note**
>
> You can also download the `angular-cookies.js` file from the AngularJS website at http://code.angularjs.org/<version>/, where <version> is the version of AngularJS that you are using. You might need to download the `angular-cookies.min.js.map` file as well, depending on which version of AngularJS you are using.

Second, you add ngCookies to the required list in your application Module definition. For example:

```
var app = angular.module('myApp', ['ngCookies']);
```

Third, you inject the $cookies or $cookieStore service into your controller. For example:

```
app.controller('myController', ['$scope', '$cookieStore',
                                function($scope, cookieStore) {
}]);
```

Listings 9.5 and 9.6 illustrate getting and setting cookies using the $cookie service. Listing 9.5 loads ngCookies in the application, injects $cookieStore into the controller, and then uses the get(), put(), and remove() methods to interact with a cookie named myAppCookie.

Listing 9.6 implements a set of radio buttons that tie to the favCookie value in the model and use ng-change to call setCookie() when the values of the buttons change. Figure 9.2 shows the resulting web page.

Listing 9.5   service_cookie.js: Implementing an AngularJS Controller That Interacts with Browser Cookies by Using the $cookieStore Service

```
01 var app = angular.module('myApp', ['ngCookies']);
02 app.controller('myController', ['$scope', '$cookieStore',
03                                 function($scope, cookieStore) {
04     $scope.favCookie = '';
05     $scope.myFavCookie = '';
06     $scope.setCookie = function(){
07       if ($scope.favCookie === 'None'){
08         cookieStore.remove('myAppCookie');
09       }else{
10         cookieStore.put('myAppCookie', {flavor:$scope.favCookie});
11       }
12       $scope.myFavCookie = cookieStore.get('myAppCookie');
13     };
14   }]);
```

Listing 9.6   service_cookie.html: An AngularJS Template That Implements Radio Buttons to Set a Cookie Value

```
01 <!doctype html>
02 <html ng-app="myApp">
03 <head>
04   <title>AngularJS $cookie Service</title>
05 </head>
06 <body>
07   <div ng-controller="myController">
08     <h3>Favorite Cookie:</h3>
```

```
09      <input type="radio" value="Chocolate Chip" ng-model="favCookie"
10             ng-change="setCookie()">Chocolate Chip</input><br>
11      <input type="radio" value="Oatmeal" ng-model="favCookie"
12             ng-change="setCookie()">Oatmeal</input><br>
13      <input type="radio" value="Frosted" ng-model="favCookie"
14             ng-change="setCookie()">Frosted</input><br>
15      <input type="radio" value="None" ng-model="favCookie"
16             ng-change="setCookie()">None</input>
17      <hr>Cookies: {{myFavCookie}}
18    </div>
19    <script src="http://code.angularjs.org/1.3.0/angular.min.js"></script>
20    <script src="http://code.angularjs.org/1.3.0/angular-cookies.min.js"></script>
21    <script src="js/service_cookie.js"></script>
22  </body>
23  </html>
```

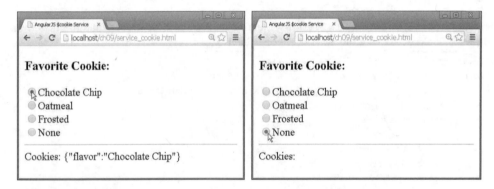

Figure 9.2   Implementing the $cookieStore service to allow AngularJS controllers to interact with the browser cookies.

Implementing Timers with $interval and $timeout Services

The AngularJS $interval and $timeout services enable you to delay execution of code for an amount of time. These services interact with the JavaScript setInterval and setTimeout functionality—but within the AngularJS framework.

The $interval and $timeout services use the following syntax:

```
$interval(callback, delay, [count], [invokeApply]);
$timeout(callback, delay, [invokeApply]);
```

The parameters are described here:

- **callback:** Is executed when the delay has expired.

- **delay:** Specifies the number of milliseconds to wait before the callback function is executed.

- **count:** Indicates the number of times to repeat the interval.

- **invokeApply:** Is a Boolean that, if `true`, causes the function to execute only in the `$apply()` block of the AngularJS event cycle. The default is `true`.

When you call the `$interval()` and `$timeout()` methods, they return a promise object that you can use to cancel the timeout or interval. To cancel an existing `$timeout` or `$interval`, call the `cancel()` method. For example:

```
var myInterval = $interval(function(){$scope.seconds++;}, 1000, 10, true);
. . .
$interval.cancel(myInterval);
```

If you create timeouts or intervals by using `$timeout` or `$interval`, you must explicitly destroy them by using `cancel()` when the `scope` or `elements` directives are destroyed. The easiest way to do this is by adding a listener to the `$destroy` event. For example:

```
$scope.$on('$destroy', function(){
  $scope.cancel(myInterval);
});
```

Using the `$animate` Service

The `$animate` service provides animation detection hooks you can use when performing enter, leave, and move DOM operations, as well as `addClass` and `removeClass` operations. You can use these hooks either through CSS classnames or through the `$animate` service in JavaScript.

To implement animation, you need to add a directive that supports animation to the element that you want to animate. Table 9.3 lists the directives that support animation and the types of animation events that they support.

Table 9.3 AngularJS Directives That Support Animation

Directive	Description
ngRepeat	Supports `enter`, `leave`, and `move` events.
ngView	Supports `enter` and `leave` events.
ngInclude	Supports `enter` and `leave` events.
ngSwitch	Supports `enter` and `leave` events.
ngIf	Supports `enter` and `leave` events.

Directive	Description
ngClass	Supports `addClass` and `removeClass` events.
ngShow	Supports `addClass` and `removeClass` events.
ngHide	Supports `addClass` and `removeClass` events.

Implementing Animation in CSS

To implement animation in CSS, you need to include the `ngClass` directive in the element that you want to animate. AngularJS uses the `ngClass` value as a root name for additional CSS classes that will be added to and removed from the element during animation.

An animation event is called on an element with an `ngClass` directive defined. Table 9.4 lists the additional classes that are added and removed during the animation process.

Table 9.4   **AngularJS Directives That Are Automatically Added and Removed During Animation**

Class	Description
`ng-animate`	Added when an event is triggered.
`ng-animate-active`	Added when animation starts and triggers CSS transitions.
`<super>-ng-move`	Added when `move` events are triggered.
`<super>-ng-move-active`	Added when move animation starts and triggers CSS transitions.
`<super>-ng-leave`	Added when `leave` events are triggered.
`<super>-ng-leave-active`	Added when leave animation starts and triggers CSS transitions.
`<super>-ng-enter`	Added when `enter` events are triggered.
`<super>-ng-enter-active`	Added when enter animation starts and triggers CSS transitions.
`<super>-ng-add`	Added when `addClass` events are triggered.
`<super>-ng-add-active`	Added when add class animation starts and triggers CSS transitions.
`<super>-ng-remove`	Added when `removeClass` events are triggered.
`<super>-ng-remove-active`	Added when remove class animation starts and triggers CSS transitions.

To implement CSS-based animations, all you need to do is add the appropriate CSS transition code for the additional classes listed in Table 9.4. To illustrate this, the following snippet implements add class and remove class transitions for a user-defined class named .img-fade that animates changing the opacity of the image to .1 for a two-second duration:

```
.img-fade-add, .img-fade-remove {
  -webkit-transition:all ease 2s;
  -moz-transition:all ease 2s;
  -o-transition:all ease 2s;
  transition:all ease 2s;
}
.img-fade, .img-fade-add.img-fade-add-active {
  opacity:.1;
}
```

Notice that the transitions are added to the .img-fade-add and .img-fade-remove classes, but the actual class definition is applied to .img-fade. You also need the class definition .img-fade-add.img-fade-add-active to set the ending state for the transition.

Implementing Animation in JavaScript

Implementing AngularJS CSS animation is very simple, but you can also implement animation in JavaScript using jQuery. JavaScript animations provide more direct control over your animations. Also, JavaScript animations do not require a browser to support CSS3.

To implement animation in JavaScript, you need to include the jQuery library in your template before the angular.js library is loaded. For example:

```
<script src="http://code.jquery.com/jquery-1.11.0.min.js"></script>
```

Note

Including the full jQuery library is necessary if you want to be able to utilize the full features of jQuery animation. If you do decide to include the jQuery library, make certain that it is loaded before the AngularJS library in your HTML code.

You also need to include the ngAnimate dependency in your application Module object definition. For example:

```
var app = angular.module('myApp', ['ngAnimate']);
```

You can then use the animate() method on your Module object to implement animations. The animate() method returns an object that provides functions for the enter, leave, move, addClass, and removeClass events that you want to handle. These functions are passed the element to be animated as the first parameter. You can then use the jQuery animate() method to animate an element.

The jQuery `animate()` method uses the following syntax, in which `cssProperties` is an object of CSS attribute changes, `duration` is specified in milliseconds, `easing` is the easing method, and `callback` is the function to execute when the animation completes:

```
animate(cssProperties, [duration], [easing], [callback])
```

For example, the following code animates adding the `fadeClass` class to an element by setting `opacity` to 0:

```
app.animation('.fadeClass', function() {
  return {
    addClass : function(element, className, done) {
      jQuery(element).animate({ opacity: 0}, 3000);
    },
  };
});
```

Animating Elements Using AngularJS

Listings 9.7, 9.8, and 9.9 implement a basic animation example that applies a fade-in/out animation to an image, using the JavaScript method, and uses CSS transition animation to animate resizing the image.

Listing 9.7 contains the AngularJS controller and animation code. Notice that the same class `.fadeOut` is used to apply both the fade-in and the fade-out animations by hooking into the `addClass` and `removeClass` events.

Listing 9.8 implements the AngularJS template that supports the animation. Notice that line 5 loads the jQuery library to support the JavaScript animation code. Also, line 6 loads the `animate.css` script that contains the transition animations shown in Listing 9.9. The buttons simply add and remove the appropriate classes to initiate the animations.

Listing 9.9 provides the necessary transition CSS definitions for the `add` and `remove` classes that get implemented during the animation process. Figure 9.3 shows the results.

Listing 9.7   `service_animate.js`: Implementing an AngularJS Controller That Implements jQuery Animation Using the `$animation` Service

```
01 var app = angular.module('myApp', ['ngAnimate']);
02 app.controller('myController', function($scope ) {
03    $scope.myImgClass = 'start-class';
04    });
05 app.animation('.fadeOut', function() {
06    return {
```

```
07    enter : function(element, parentElement, afterElement, doneCallback) {},
08    leave : function(element, doneCallback) {},
09    move : function(element, parentElement, afterElement, doneCallback) {},
10    addClass : function(element, className, done) {
11      jQuery(element).animate({ opacity: 0}, 3000);
12    },
13    removeClass : function(element, className, done) {
14      jQuery(element).animate({ opacity: 1}, 3000);
15    }
16  };
17 });
```

Listing 9.8 `service_animate.html`: An AngularJS Template That Implements Buttons That Change the Class on an Image to Animate Fading and Resizing

```
01 <!doctype html>
02 <html ng-app="myApp">
03 <head>
04   <title>AngularJS $animate Service</title>
05   <link rel="stylesheet" href="css/animate.css">
06 </head>
07 <body>
08   <div ng-controller="myController">
09     <h3>AngularJS Image Animation:</h3>
10     <input type="button"
11           ng-click="myImgClass='fadeOut'" value="Fade Out"/>
12     <input type="button"
13           ng-click="myImgClass=''" value="Fade In"/>
14     <input type="button"
15           ng-click="myImgClass='shrink'" value="Small"/>
16     <input type="button"
17           ng-click="myImgClass='grow'" value="Big"/>
18     <hr>
19     <img ng-class="myImgClass" src="/images/canyon.jpg" />
20   </div>
21   <script src="http://code.jquery.com/jquery-1.11.0.min.js"></script>
22   <script src="http://code.angularjs.org/1.3.0/angular.min.js"></script>
23   <script
➥src="http://code.angularjs.org/1.3.0/angular-animate.min.js"></script>
24   <script src="js/service_animate.js"></script>
25 </body>
26 </html>
```

> **Note**
>
> You can also download the `angular-animate.js` file from the AngularJS website at http://code.angularjs.org/<version>/, where *version* is the version of AngularJS that you are using. You might need to download the `angular-animate.min.js.map` file as well, depending on which version of AngularJS you are using.

Listing 9.9   `animate.css`: **CSS Code That Provides Transition Effects for the Various Class Stages of the AngularJS Animation Code**

```
01 .shrink-add, .grow-add {
02   -webkit-transition:all ease 2.5s;
03   -moz-transition:all ease 2.5s;
04   -o-transition:all ease 2.5s;
05   transition:all ease 2.5s;
06 }
07 .shrink,
08 .shrink-add.shrink-add-active {
09   width:100px;
10 }
11 .start-class,
12 .grow,
13 .grow-add.grow-add-active {
14   width:400px;
15 }
```

Figure 9.3 Implementing the $animation service in both CSS and JavaScript to animate fading and resizing an image.

Using the `$location` Service

The `$location` service provides a wrapper to the JavaScript `window.location` object. This makes the URL accessible in your AngularJS application. Not only can you get information about the URL, but you also can modify it, changing the location with a new URL or navigating to a specific hash tag.

To add the `$location` service to a controller or service, you simply need to inject it using the standard dependency injection methods. For example:

```
app.controller('myController', ['$scope', '$location',
                            function($scope, location) {
    . . .
  }]);
```

Table 9.5 lists the methods that can be called on the `$location` service and describes their implementation.

Table 9.5   **Methods Available on the AngularJS `$location` Service Object**

Method	Description
absUrl()	Returns the full URL that was passed to the browser.

url([*url*])	Returns the URL that was passed to the browser if called with no parameters, for example:
	
	`location.url()`
	
	Adding a *url* parameter to the url() method will set the current relative URL for the location. For example:
	
	`location.url("/new/path?new=query")`

protocol()	Returns the protocol that was used in the current URL.
host()	Returns the host that was used in the current URL.
port()	Returns the port that was used in the current URL.

path([*path*])	Returns the protocol that was used in the current URL if no parameters are passed, for example:
	
	`location.path()`
	
	Adding a *path* parameter to the path() method will set the current relative path for the location. For example:
	
	`location.path("/new/path ")`

Method	Description

`search([search], [paramValue])`	Returns a JavaScript object containing the query parameters passed as part of the URL if no `search` or `paramValue` parameter is passed to the `search()` function, for example:
	`location.search()`
	
	If you pass `search` and `paramValue` parameters, then the value of the parameter named by `search` will be changed in the URL to the value specified by `paramValue`. For example:
	
	`location.search("param1", "newValue")`

`hash()`	Returns the hashtag that was used in the current URL.
`replace()`	When you call this on the `$location` service object, all subsequent changes to the location will replace the history record instead of adding a new one.

The code in Listings 9.10 and 9.11 implement a simple example of using the `$location` service to access and change elements in the URL passed to the browser. The code in Listing 9.10 implements a controller that is injected with the `$location` service. The function `updateLocationInfo()` gets the `url`, `absUrl`, `host`, `protocol`, `path`, `search`, and `hash` values from the `$location` service. The `changePath()`, `changeHash()`, and `changeSearch()` functions change the path, hash, and search values in the location and then update the scope with the new values.

The code in Listing 9.11 implements an AngularJS template that displays the captured `$location` service information and provides links to change the `path`, `hash`, and `search` properties. Figure 9.4 shows the web page in action. Notice that when the links are clicked the `path`, `hash`, and `search` values change.

Listing 9.10   `service_location.js`: An AngularJS Application That Implements a Controller to Gather Information from the `$location` Service and Provides Functions to Change the `path`, `search`, and `hash` Values

```
01 var app = angular.module('myApp', []);
02 app.controller('myController', ['$scope', '$location',
03                                 function($scope, location) {
04   $scope.updateLocationInfo = function() {
05     $scope.url = location.url();
06     $scope.absUrl = location.absUrl();
07     $scope.host = location.host();
08     $scope.port = location.port();
09     $scope.protocol = location.protocol();
```

```
10      $scope.path = location.path();
11      $scope.search = location.search();
12      $scope.hash = location.hash();
13    };
14    $scope.changePath = function(){
15      location.path("/new/path");
16      $scope.updateLocationInfo();
17    };
18    $scope.changeHash = function(){
19      location.hash("newHash");
20      $scope.updateLocationInfo();
21    };
22    $scope.changeSearch = function(){
23      location.search("p1", "newA");
24      $scope.updateLocationInfo();
25    };
26    $scope.updateLocationInfo();
27  }]);
```

Listing 9.11 `service_location.html`: An AngularJS Template That Displays Information Gathered from the `$location` Service and Provides Links to Change the `path`, `search`, and `hash` Values

```
01 <!doctype html>
02 <html ng-app="myApp">
03 <head>
04   <title>AngularJS $location Service</title>
05   <style>
06     span {
07       color: red; text-decoration: underline;
08       cursor: pointer; }
09   </style>
10 </head>
11 <body>
12   <div ng-controller="myController">
13     <h3>Location Service:</h3>
14     [<span ng-click="changePath()">Change Path</span>]
15     [<span ng-click="changeHash()">Change Hash</span>]
16     [<span ng-click="changeSearch()">Change Search</span>]
17     <hr>
18     <h4>URL Info</h4>
19     url: {{url}}<br>
20     absUrl: {{absUrl}}<br>
21     host: {{host}}<br>
22     port: {{port}}<br>
23     protocol: {{protocol}}<br>
```

```
24      path: {{path}}<br>
25      search: {{search}}<br>
26      hash: {{hash}}<br>
27    </div>
28    <script src="http://code.angularjs.org/1.3.0/angular.min.js"></script>
29    <script src="js/service_location.js"></script>
30  </body>
31  </html>
```

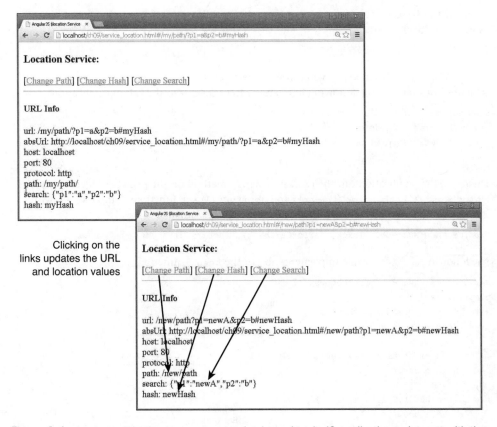

Clicking on the links updates the URL and location values

Figure 9.4   Implementing the `$location` service in an AngularJS application to interact with the browser location.

Using the $q Service to Provide Deferred Responses

An extremely useful service provided by AngularJS is the $q service. The $q service is a promise/deferred response implementation. Since not all services can respond immediately to a request, there is a need to defer the response until the service is ready to respond. That is where the $q service comes in. The idea is that you can make a request, and rather than getting the response directly, you will get a promise that the service will respond. The requesting application can then assign a callback function that should be executed when the deferred request completes successfully or fails.

To utilize the $q service for deferred responses, you will first need to create a deferred object using the following syntax:

```
var deferred = $q.defer();
```

After you have a deferred object, you can pass the promise around by accessing the promise attribute. For example, the following line returns the promise to the calling application:

```
function makeDeferredRequest(){
  var deferred = $q.defer();
  return deferred.promise;
}
```

The requesting application can then call the then() method on the promise object to register successCallback, errorCallback, and notifyCallback functions using the following syntax:

```
promise.then(successCallback, [errorCallback], [notifyCallback])
```

The following shows a sample implementation of the then() function:

```
var promise = makeDeferredRequest();
promise.then(
  function successCallback(value){
    //handle success
  },
  function errorCallback(value){
    //handle error
  },
  function notifyCallback(value){
    //handle notify
  },
```

From the deferred service side you can use the methods described in Table 9.6 to handle notifying the requesting application of the status of the request.

Table 9.6   **Methods Available on a Deferred Object of the $q Service**

Service	Description
$resolve(value)	Executes the successCallback function on the promise object and passes the value specified to it.
$reject(reason)	Executes the errorCallback function on the promise object and passes the reason specified to it.
$notify(value)	Executes the notifyCallback function on the promise object and passes the value specified to it.

The "Implementing a Database Access Service" section of Chapter 10, "Creating Your Own Custom AngularJS Services," shows a good example of using the $q service to handle the deferred responses to remote database requests.

Summary

AngularJS services are singleton objects that you can register with the dependency injector; controllers and other AngularJS components, including other services, can consume them. AngularJS provides much of the back-end functionality in the way of services, such as $http, which enables you to easily integrate web server communication into your AngularJS applications.

In this chapter you also learned about several of the built-in services, such as $cookieStore, $q, $window, $location, $animate, and $cacheFactory. These and other AngularJS services can be used to easily inject functionality into your controllers, directives, and custom services.

Creating Your Own Custom AngularJS Services

AngularJS provides a lot of functionality in built-in services; however, you will also need to be able to implement your own custom services that provide your own specific functionality. You should implement a custom service anytime you need to provide task-based functionality to your applications.

When implementing custom services, you need to think about the service as a chunk of reusable code that performs one or more related tasks. Then you can design and group them together into custom modules that can easily be consumed by several different AngularJS applications.

This chapter introduces the AngularJS custom services. Then the chapter provides several examples of custom AngularJS service implementation to provide you with a clearer understanding of how to design and build your own.

Understanding Custom AngularJS Services

AngularJS enables you to create your own custom services to provide functionality in AngularJS components that require it. As you saw in the previous chapter, the built-in AngularJS services provide a wide variety of functionality for AngularJS applications. Using custom services, you can customize, enhance, and extend that functionality in many ways.

There are four main types of services that you will likely be implementing in your code: `value`, `constant`, `factory`, and `service`. The following sections cover these services.

Defining a `value` Service

You use the very simple `value` service to define a single value that you can inject as a service provider. The `value` method uses the following syntax, where `name` is the service name and `object` is any JavaScript object you want to provide:

```
value(name, object)
```

For example:

```
var app = angular.module('myApp', []);
app.value('myValue', {color:'blue', value:'17'});
```

Defining a `constant` Service

The `constant` service is basically the same as the `value` service, except that `constant` services are available in the configuration phase of building the `Module` object, whereas `value` services are not. The `constant` method uses the following syntax, where `name` is the service name and `object` is any JavaScript object you want to provide:

```
constant(name, object)
```

For example:

```
var app = angular.module('myApp', []);
app.constant('myConst', "Constant String");
```

Using a Factory Provider to Build a `factory` Service

The `factory` method provides the capability to implement functionality into a service. It can also be dependent on other service providers, enabling you to build up compartmentalized code. The `factory` method uses the following syntax, where `name` is the service name and `factoryProvider` is a provider function that builds the factory service:

```
factory(name, factoryProvider)
```

You can inject the `factory` method with other services, and it returns the service object with the appropriate functionality. The functionality can be a complex JavaScript service, a value, or a simple function. For example, the following code implements a `factory` service that returns a function that adds two numbers:

```
var app = angular.module('myApp', []);
app.constant('myConst', 10);
app.factory('multiplier', ['myConst', function (myConst) {
  return function(value) { return value + myConst; };
}]);
```

Using an Object to Define a `service` Service

The `service` method provides the capability to implement functionality into a server. However, the `service` method works slightly differently than the `factory` method. The `service` method accepts a constructor function as the second argument and uses it to create a new instance of an object. The `service` method uses the following syntax, where `name` is the service name and `constructor` is a constructor function:

```
service(name, constructor)
```

The `service` method can also accept dependency injection. The following code implements a basic service method that provides an `add()` function and a `multiply()` function:

```
var app = angular.module('myApp', []);
app.constant('myConst', 10);
function ConstMathObj(myConst) {
  this.add = function(value){ return value + myConst; };
  this.multiply = function(value){ return value * myConst; };
}
app.service('constMath', ['myConst', ConstMathObj] );
```

Notice that the `ConstMathObj` constructor is created first, and then the `service()` method calls it and uses dependency injection to insert the `myConst` service.

Integrating Custom Services into Your AngularJS Applications

As you begin implementing AngularJS services for your applications, you will find that some will be very simplistic and others will become very complex. The complexity of the service typically reflects the complexity of the underlying data and functionality that it provides. The purpose of this section is to provide you with some basic examples of different types of custom services to illustrate how they can be implemented and utilized.

Each of the following sections contains an example to illustrate different aspects of custom services. The first is designed to show you how to implement the different types of services. The second is designed to show you the reusability of services. The third is designed to show you a different look into service interactions.

Implementing a Simple Application That Uses All Four Types of Services

In this example you will build `constant`, `value`, `factory`, and `service` services. The purpose is to give a chance to see how each can be implemented, as well as the perspective of using multiple types of services in your applications.

The code in Listing 10.1 shows an example of integrating `value`, `constant`, `factory`, and `service` services into a single module. The example is very basic and easy to follow. Notice that `censorWords` and `repString` are injected into and used in the `factory` and `service` definitions.

Lines 4–13 implement a `factory` service that returns a function that censors a string. Notice that line 26 calls the `factory` directly to censor the string.

Lines 14–25 implement a `service` service by first defining the `CensorObj` object constructor and then, on line 26, registering the service to the application. The `CensorObj` object defines two functions: `censor()`, which censors the words in a string, and `censoredWords()`, which returns the words that will be censored.

In lines 27 and 28 the `censorS` and `censorF` services are injected into a controller. The controller then can utilize the custom services by calling `censorF()` directly in line 34 and calling `censorS.censor()` in line 35.

The code in Listing 10.2 implements an AngularJS template that displays the censored words and provides a text input to type in a phrase. The phrase is displayed twice, once censored by `censorF` and once by `censorS`. Figure 10.1 shows the AngularJS application in action.

Listing 10.1 `service_custom_censor.js`: Implementing and Consuming Multiple Custom Services in an AngularJS Controller

```
01 var app = angular.module('myApp', []);
02 app.value('censorWords', ["can't", "quit", "fail"]);
03 app.constant('repString', "****");
04 app.factory('censorF', ['censorWords', 'repString',
05                          function (cWords, repString) {
06   return function(inString) {
07     var outString = inString;
08     for(i in cWords){
09       outString = outString.replace(cWords[i], repString);
10     }
11     return outString;
12   };
13 }]);
14 function CensorObj(cWords, repString) {
15   this.censor = function(inString){
16     var outString = inString;
17     for(i in cWords){
18       outString = outString.replace(cWords[i], repString);
19     }
20     return outString;
21   };
22   this.censoredWords = function(){
23     return cWords;
24   };
25 }
26 app.service('censorS', ['censorWords', 'repString', CensorObj]);
27 app.controller('myController', ['$scope', 'censorF', 'censorS',
28                                 function($scope, censorF, censorS) {
29   $scope.censoredWords = censorS.censoredWords();
```

```
30   $scope.inPhrase = "";
31   $scope.censoredByFactory = censorF("");
32   $scope.censoredByService = censorS.censor("");;
33   $scope.$watch('inPhrase', function(newValue, oldValue){
34      $scope.censoredByFactory = censorF(newValue);
35      $scope.censoredByService = censorS.censor(newValue);
36   });
37 }]);
```

Listing 10.2 `service_custom_sensor.html`: AngularJS Template That Illustrates the
Interaction of Multiple Custom Services in an AngularJS Controller

```
01 <!doctype html>
02 <html ng-app="myApp">
03 <head>
04   <title>AngularJS Custom Censor Service</title>
05   <style>
06     p { color: red; margin-left: 15px; }
07     input { width: 250px; }
08   </style>
09 </head>
10 <body>
11   <div ng-controller="myController">
12      <h3>Custom Censor Service:</h3>
13      Censored Words:<br>
14      <p>{{censoredWords|json}}</p>
15      <hr>
16      Enter Phrase:<br>
17      <input type="text" ng-model="inPhrase" /><hr>
18      Filtered by Factory:
19      <p>{{censoredByFactory}}</p>
20      Filtered by Service:
21      <p>{{censoredByService}}</p>
22   </div>
23   <script src="http://code.angularjs.org/1.3.0/angular.min.js"></script>
24   <script src="js/service_custom_censor.js"></script>
25 </body>
26 </html>
```

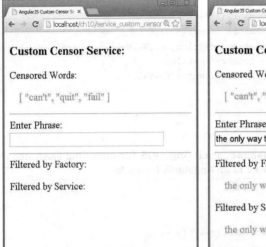
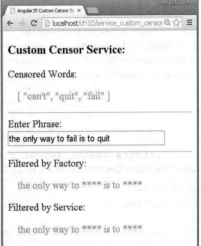

Figure 10.1   Using multiple custom services in an AngularJS controller to censor words in a phrase.

Implementing Simple Time Service

In this example you will build a simple time service that generates a local time object for different cities. Then in the AngularJS template you will use the time service in multiple controllers. The purpose is to give you a chance to see how easy it is to reuse an AngularJS service.

The code in Listing 10.3 implements a custom service named `TimeService` using the function `TimeObj()` to generate the service object. The code in `TimeObj` simply defines a list of cities with a time zone offset and provides the `getTZDate()` function to return a JavaScript Date object for a specific city. The `getCities()` function creates an array of the cities represented and returns it.

Notice that there are several controllers added to the application, including `LAController`, `NYController`, `LondonController`, and `TimeController`. These controllers are injected with the `TimeService` service and use it to set the current time for a city or, in the case of `TimeController`, all cities.

The code in Listing 10.4 implements an AngularJS template that displays the time for the `LAController`, `NYController`, `LondonController`, and `TimeController` controllers. In the case of `TimeController`, all times are displayed in a table using `ng-repeat`.

Figure 10.2 shows the resulting AngularJS application web page. Notice the different times represented.

Listing 10.3   `service_custom_time.js`: Implementing and Consuming a Custom AngularJS Service in Multiple Controllers

```
01 var app = angular.module('myApp', []);
02 function TimeObj() {
03   var cities = { 'Los Angeles': -8,
04                  'New York': -5,
05                  'London': 0,
06                  'Paris': 1,
07                  'Tokyo': 9 };
08   this.getTZDate = function(city){
09     var localDate = new Date();
10     var utcTime = localDate.getTime() +
11                   localDate.getTimezoneOffset() *
12                   60*1000;
13     return new Date(utcTime +
14                  (60*60*1000 *
15                   cities[city]));
16   };
17   this.getCities = function(){
18     var cList = [];
19     for (var key in cities){
20       cList.push(key);
21     }
22     return cList;
23   };
24 }
25 app.service('TimeService', [TimeObj]);
26 app.controller('LAController', ['$scope', 'TimeService',
```

```
27                        function($scope, timeS) {
28    $scope.myTime = timeS.getTZDate("Los Angeles").toLocaleTimeString();
29 }]);
30 app.controller('NYController', ['$scope', 'TimeService',
31                        function($scope, timeS) {
32    $scope.myTime = timeS.getTZDate("New York").toLocaleTimeString();
33 }]);
34 app.controller('LondonController', ['$scope', 'TimeService',
35                        function($scope, timeS) {
36    $scope.myTime = timeS.getTZDate("London").toLocaleTimeString();
37 }]);
38 app.controller('TimeController', ['$scope', 'TimeService',
39                        function($scope, timeS) {
40    $scope.cities = timeS.getCities();
41    $scope.getTime = function(cityName){
42      return timeS.getTZDate(cityName).toLocaleTimeString();
43    };
44 }]);
```

Listing 10.4　`service_custom_time.html`: AngularJS Template That Illustrates Injecting a Custom AngularJS Service into Multiple Controllers

```
01 <!doctype html>
02 <html ng-app="myApp">
03 <head>
04   <title>AngularJS Custom Time Service</title>
05   <style>
06     span {
07       color: lightgreen; background-color: black;
08       border: 3px ridge; padding: 2px;
09       font: 14px/18px arial, serif; }
10   </style>
11 </head>
12 <body>
13   <h2>Custom Time Service:</h2><hr>
14   <div ng-controller="LAController">
15     Los Angeles Time:
16     <span>{{myTime}}</span>
17   </div><hr>
18   <div ng-controller="NYController">
19     New York Time:
20     <span>{{myTime}}</span>
21   </div><hr>
22   <div ng-controller="LondonController">
23     London Time:
24     <span>{{myTime}}</span>
```

```
25  </div><hr>
26  <div ng-controller="TimeController">
27    All Times:
28    <table>
29    <tr>
30        <th ng-repeat="city in cities">
31          {{city}}
32        </th>
33    </tr>
34    <tr>
35        <td ng-repeat="city in cities">
36          <span>{{getTime(city)}}</span>
37        </td>
38    </tr>
39    </table>
40  </div><hr>
41    <script src="http://code.angularjs.org/1.3.0/angular.min.js"></script>
42    <script src="js/service_custom_time.js"></script>
43  </body>
44  </html>
```

Figure 10.2   Using a custom AngularJS service in multiple controllers to display the time for different cities.

Implementing a Database Access Service

In this example you will build an intermediate database access service that uses the `$http` service to connect to a simple Node.js server that will act as a server-side database service. The purpose of this exercise is to illustrate the usage of built-in services alongside custom services. This also gives a good example of utilizing the `$q` service.

Listing 10.5 implements the Node.js web server that handles the following GET and POST routes to get and set a user object and an array of table data to simulate making requests to a remote database service:

- **/get/user:** A GET route that returns the JSON version of a user object.

- **/get/data:** A GET route that returns the JSON version of an array of table data.

- **/set/user:** A POST route that accepts a user object in the body of the request and updates the object on the server to simulate storing a user object.

- **/set/data:** A POST route that accepts an array of objects in the body of the request and updates the data variable to simulate storing database data. Typically, you would never store all the table data at once but for simplicity of this example this is how it is.

You don't necessarily need to pay a lot of attention to the code in Listing 10.5 other than understanding the routes that it provides so that you can follow the interactions in the AngularJS application defined in Listings 10.6, 10.7, and 10.8. The server is very rudimentary, doesn't handle errors, and just dynamically generates data to simulate the database.

> ### Note
>
> You will need to stop the normal `server.js` HTTP server if it is running before starting `service_server.js` from Listing 10.5. Also, you will want to place the `service_db_server.js` file from Listing 10.5 in the parent folder to the `service_db_access.html` in Listing 10.6 for the paths to match up properly in the Node.js static routes. The structure should look similar to this:
>
> ```
> ./service_db_server.js
> ./ch10/service_custom_db.html
> ./ch09/js/service_custom_db_access.js
> ./ch09/js/service_custom_db.js
> ```

Listing 10.5 `service_db_server.js`: Implementing a Node.js Express Server That Supports GET and POST Routes to Simulate a Database Service for the AngularJS Controller

```
01 var express = require('express');
02 var bodyParser = require('body-parser');
03 var app = express();
04 app.use('/', express.static('./'));
05 app.use(bodyParser.urlencoded({ extended: true }));
06 app.use(bodyParser.json());
07 var user = {
```

```
08                first: 'Christopher',
09                last: 'Columbus',
10                username: 'cc1492',
11                title: 'Admiral',
12                home: 'Genoa'
13            };
14 var data = [];
15 function r(min, max){
16   var n = Math.floor(Math.random() * (max - min + 1)) + min;
17   if (n<10){ return '0' + n; }
18   else { return n; }
19 }
20 function p(start, end, total, current){
21   return Math.floor((end-start)*(current/total)) + start;
22 }
23 function d(plusDays){
24   var start = new Date(1492, 7, 3);
25   var current = new Date(1492, 7, 3);
26   current.setDate(start.getDate()+plusDays);
27   return current.toDateString();
28 }
29 function makeData(){
30   var t = 70;
31   for (var x=0; x < t; x++){
32     var entry = {
33       day: d(x),
34       time: r(0, 23) + ':' + r(0, 59),
35       longitude: p(37, 25, t, x) + '\u00B0 '+ r(0,59) + ' N',
36       latitude: p(6, 77, t, x) + '\u00B0 '+ r(0,59) + ' W'
37     };
38     data.push(entry);
39   }
40 }
41 makeData();
42 app.get('/get/user', function(req, res){
43   res.json(user);
44 });
45 app.get('/get/data', function(req, res){
46   res.json(data);
47 });
48 app.post('/set/user', function(req, res){
49   console.log(req.body.userData);
50   user = req.body.userData;
51   res.json({ data: user, status: "User Updated." });
52 });
53 app.post('/set/data', function(req, res){
54   data = req.body.data;
```

```
55   res.json({ data: data, status: "Data Updated." });
56 });
57 app.listen(80);
```

The code in Listing 10.6 implements a module named dbAccess and a custom service named
DBService. The DBAccessObj() function that creates the service object provides the
getUserData() and updateUser() methods to retrieve and update the user object from the
server using $http requests. The getData and updateData() methods provide similar func-
tionality for the table data. Notice how the $q service is used to defer the response to the $http
requests since the request will not return immediately.

The code in Listing 10.7 implements the application module. Notice that on line 1 the
dbAccess module is injected into the myApp module to provide access to the DBService
service. DBService is injected into the controller on line 2 and then used on lines 6, 12, 18,
and 23 to make calls to get and set data from the server and assign it to the $scope.userInfo
and $scope.data values in the scope. Notice how the $q service then() function is used to
handle the deferred responses. For simplicity only the successCallback function is implemented. Normally you would also want to implement an errorCallback function as well.

The code in Listing 10.8 implements an AngularJS template that displays the user info in text
inputs and binds the values directly to the scope. There are also two input buttons that call
updateUser() to update the user info on the server and getUser() to refresh the scope data
from the server. Similarly, there are two input buttons that call updateData() and getData()
to provide the same functionality for updating and refreshing the table data from the model.

Figure 10.3 shows the rendered AngularJS web application working. When you click on the
Update User or Update Data buttons, the values are changed on the server. That means that
you can reload the web page and even exit the browser and come back, and the values will still
be the updated versions.

Listing 10.6   `service_custom_db_access.js`: Implementing a Custom AngularJS Service That Utilizes the `$http` and `$q` Services to Provide Interaction with Data Stored on the Server

```
01 var app = angular.module('dbAccess', []);
02 function DBAccessObj($http, $q) {
03   this.getUserData = function(){
04     var deferred = $q.defer();
05     $http.get('/get/user')
06     .success(function(response, status, headers, config) {
07       deferred.resolve(response);
08     });
09     return deferred.promise;
10   };
11   this.updateUser = function(userInfo){
12     var deferred = $q.defer();
13     $http.post('/set/user', { userData: userInfo}).
14     success(function(response, status, headers, config) {
```

```
15      deferred.resolve(response);
16    });
17    return deferred.promise;
18  };
19  this.getData = function(){
20    var deferred = $q.defer();
21    $http.get('/get/data')
22    .success(function(response, status, headers, config) {
23      deferred.resolve(response);
24    });
25    return deferred.promise;
26  };
27  this.updateData = function(data){
28    var deferred = $q.defer();
29    $http.post('/set/data', { data: data}).
30    success(function(response, status, headers, config) {
31      deferred.resolve(response);
32    });
33    return deferred.promise;
34  };
35 }
36 app.service('DBService', ['$http', '$q', DBAccessObj]);
```

Listing 10.7 `service_custom_db.js`: Implementing an AngularJS Application That Injects the Module and Service from Listing 10.6 to Utilize the Database Access Service

```
01 var app = angular.module('myApp', ['dbAccess']);
02 app.controller('myController', ['$scope', 'DBService',
03                                 function($scope, db) {
04   $scope.status = "";
05   $scope.getUser = function(){
06     db.getUserData().then(function(response){
07       $scope.userInfo = response;
08       $scope.status = "User Data Retrieve.";
09     });
10   };
11   $scope.getData = function(){
12     db.getData().then(function(response){
13       $scope.data = response;
14       $scope.status = "User Data Retrieve.";
15     });
16   };
17   $scope.updateUser = function(){
18     db.updateUser($scope.userInfo).then(function(response){
19       $scope.status = response.status;
20     });
```

```
21    };
22    $scope.updateData = function(){
23      db.updateData($scope.data).then(function(response){
24        $scope.status = response.status;
25      });
26    };
27    $scope.getUser();
28    $scope.getData();
29 }]);
```

Listing 10.8 `service_custom_sensor.html`: AngularJS Template That Uses a Series of
`<input>` Elements to Display and Update Data Retrieved from the Server

```
01 <!doctype html>
02 <html ng-app="myApp">
03 <head>
04   <title>AngularJS Custom Database Service</title>
05     <style>
06       label {
07         display: inline-block; width: 75px; text-align: right; }
08       td, tr {
09         width: 125px; text-align: right; }
10       p {
11         color: red; font: italic 12px/14px; margin: 0px;}
12       h3 {
13         margin: 5px; }
14     </style>
15 </head>
16 <body>
17   <h2>Custom Database Service:</h2>
18   <div ng-controller="myController">
19     <h3>User Info:</h3>
20     <label>First:</label>
21       <input type="text" ng-model="userInfo.first" /><br>
22     <label>Last:</label>
23       <input type="text" ng-model="userInfo.last" /><br>
24     <label>Username:</label>
25       <input type="text" ng-model="userInfo.username" /><br>
26     <label>Title:</label>
27       <input type="text" ng-model="userInfo.title" /><br>
28     <label>Home:</label>
29       <input type="text" ng-model="userInfo.home" /><br>
30     <input type= button ng-click="updateUser()" value="Update User" />
31     <input type= button ng-click="getUser()" value="Refresh User Info" />
32     <hr>
33     <p>{{status}}</p>
34     <hr>
```

```
35    <h3>Data:</h3>
36    <input type= button ng-click="updateData()" value="Update Data" />
37    <input type= button ng-click="getData()" value="Refresh Data Table" /><br>
38    <table>
39      <tr><th>Day</th><th>Time</th><th>Latitude</th><th>Longitude</th></tr>
40      <tr ng-repeat="datum in data">
41        <th>{{datum.day}}</th>
42        <td><input type="text" ng-model="datum.time" /></td>
43        <td><input type="text" ng-model="datum.latitude" /></td>
44        <td><input type="text" ng-model="datum.longitude" /></td>
45      </tr>
46    </table>
47    <hr>
48  </div>
49  <script src="http://code.angularjs.org/1.3.0/angular.min.js"></script>
50  <script src="js/service_custom_db_access.js"></script>
51  <script src="js/service_custom_db.js"></script>
52 </body>
53 </html>
```

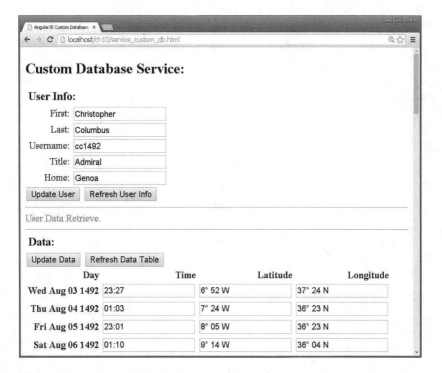

Figure 10.3   Using custom AngularJS services that implement $http to provide access to retrieve and update data on the server.

Summary

AngularJS custom services are singleton objects that you can register with the dependency injector. After they're registered with the dependency injector, controllers, directives, and other AngularJS components, including other services, can consume them. AngularJS provides several methods for creating custom services, with varying levels of complexity. The `value` and `constant` methods create simple services. On the other hand, the `factory` and `service` methods enable you to create much more complex services.

This chapter focused on the tools to enable you to implement your own custom AngularJS services when you need to provide task-based functionality to your applications. You learned about the four methods or types of custom AngularJS services, including `value`, `constant`, `factory`, and `service`.

This chapter showed examples of implementing each of the types of custom AngularJS services. You also were shown an example of implementing a custom AngularJS service in multiple controllers. The final example in this chapter showed you how to implement a standalone custom AngularJS service that interacts with the server using `$http` and how to inject and use it in another module.

Creating Rich Web Application Components the AngularJS Way

The first ten chapters of this book have been directed toward teaching you the mechanics and basic implementation of the different components of AngularJS applications. You've learned about scope/model, views, controllers, directives, and services. This chapter switches gears a bit and just provides some examples to help solidify how things are done in AngularJS.

AngularJS expects a lot more structure than normal JavaScript or even jQuery requires. However, that being said, it still provides a lot of flexibility within the framework. Consequently, it is a good idea to look at as many different angles of doing things in AngularJS as possible.

The examples in this chapter are not polished—some more than others—however, they do provide a lot of different looks at implementing custom directives and utilizing the built-in directives. The purpose is not to provide you with instantly reusable code, but to give you some different looks and have a basic framework that you can build on as you design your own implementations.

For this chapter the code files used are listed at the beginning of the section to make it easy for you to follow if you have downloaded the code from the book's website.

Building a Tabbed View

In this example you will build two custom AngularJS directives, one that acts as a tab group and the other that acts as the individual panes in the tabbed group. The objective of this example is to give you a look at nesting custom directives inside each other, as well as some communication between the two.

The folder structure for this example is as follows:

- **./server.js:** Node.js web server that serves the static project files.

- **./images:** Folder that contains the images used in the examples.

- **./ch11:** Project folder.

- **./ch11/tabbable.html:** AngularJS template for the project.

- **./ch11/tabs.html:** AngularJS partial template for the tabbed group.

- **./ch11/panel.html:** AngularJS partial template for each individual panel in the tabbed group.

- **./ch11/js/tabbable.js:** AngularJS application supporting the custom tabs directives.

The code in Listing 11.1 shows the `tabbable.js` AngularJS application that defines the two directives `myTabs` and `myPane`. Note that the HTML used inside the templates comes from the partial files using the `templateUrl` option in the directive definition. Also note that the transclude option is used, which enables us to keep the contents for the `myPane` elements in the AngularJS template.

Communication between the two directives is made possible by requiring the `myTabs` directive in the definition for `myPane`. This causes the controller defined in `myTabs` to be passed in to the link function of `myPane`. Note that on line 30 we are able to call `addPane()` to add the scope for the `myPane` directive to a list in the `myTabs` directive. The visible tab is changed using the `select()` method in the `myTabs` controller function.

Listing 11.1 `tabbable.js`: AngularJS Application That Defines Two Custom Directives That Can Be Nested to Provide a Tabbed Panel View

```
01 var app = angular.module('myApp', []);
02 app.directive('myTabs', function() {
03   return {
04     restrict: 'E',
05     transclude: true,
06     scope: {},
07     controller: function($scope) {
08       var panes = $scope.panes = [];
09       $scope.select = function(pane) {
10         angular.forEach(panes, function(pane) {
11           pane.selected = false;
12         });
13         pane.selected = true;
14       };
15       this.addPane = function(pane) {
16         if (panes.length == 0) {
17           $scope.select(pane);
18         }
19         panes.push(pane);
```

```
20      };
21    },
22    templateUrl: 'tabs.html'
23  };
24 });
25 app.directive('myPane', function() {
26   return { require: '^myTabs', restrict: 'E',
27     templateUrl: 'pane.html',
28     transclude: true, scope: { title: '@' },
29     link: function(scope, element, attrs, tabsCtrl) {
30       tabsCtrl.addPane(scope);
31     }
32   };
33 });
```

The code in Listing 11.2 contains the AngularJS partial template that acts as the replacement for the myTabs directive. Notice that the panes value in the scope is used to add the tabs as <span> elements to the top of the view. The panes array is built as each myPane element is compiled and linked into the template.

Listing 11.2   **tabs.html: AngularJS Partial Template That Contains the Template Code to Build the Tabs Container**

```
01 <div class="tabbable">
02   <div class="tabs">
03     <span class="tab" ng-repeat="pane in panes"
04         ng-class="{activeTab:pane.selected}"
05         ng-click="select(pane)">{{pane.title}}
06     </span>
07   </div>
08   <div class="tabcontent" ng-transclude></div>
09 </div>?
```

The code in Listing 11.3 contains the AngularJS partial template that acts as the replacement for the myPane directive. Notice that we use ng-show to show and hide the panes as they are clicked on. The ng-transclude attribute ensures that the contents defined in the myPane element are included in the rendered view.

Listing 11.3   **pane.html: AngularJS Partial Template That Contains the Template Code to Build the Individual Panes of the Tabbed Container**

```
01 <div class="pane"
02     ng-show="selected"
03     ng-transclude>
04 </div>
```

Listing 11.4 shows the AngularJS template that supports the `myTabs` and `myPane` directives. Note the naming structure of `my-tabs` and `my-pane` for the elements needed in the template. For this example only images are placed inside the `myPane` element. This could just as easily be a complex series of elements such as a form or table.

Figure 11.1 shows the working web page. Notice that as the tab for each pane is clicked, the content changes.

Listing 11.4   `tabbable.html`: AngularJS Template That Implements the `myTabs` and `myPane` Custom Directives to Create a Tabbed View

```
01  <!doctype html>
02  <html ng-app="myApp">
03  <head>
04    <title>Tab and Tab Pane Directives</title>
05    <style>
06      .tab{
07        display:inline-block; width:100px;
08        border-radius: .5em .5em 0 0; border:1px solid black;
09        text-align:center; font: 15px/28px Helvetica, sans-serif;
10        background-image: linear-gradient(#CCCCCC, #EEEEEE);
11        cursor: pointer; }
12      .activeTab{
13        border-bottom: none;
14        background-image: linear-gradient(#66CCFF, #CCFFFF); }
15      .pane{
16        border:1px solid black; background-color: #CCFFFF;
17        height:300px; width:400px;
18        padding:10px;  margin-top:-2px;
19        overflow: scroll; }
20    </style>
21  </head>
22  <body>
23    <h2>AngularJS Custom Tabs</h2>
24    <my-tabs>
25      <my-pane title="Canyon">
26        <img src="/images/canyon.jpg" />
27      </my-pane>
28      <my-pane title="Lake">
29        <img src="/images/lake.jpg" />
30      </my-pane>
31      <my-pane title="Sunset">
32        <img src="/images/jump.jpg" />
33      </my-pane>
34    </my-tabs>
35    <script src="http://code.angularjs.org/1.3.0/angular.min.js"></script>
```

```
36   <script src="js/tabbable.js"></script>
37 </body>
38 </html>
```

Figure 11.1   Implementing nested custom AngularJS directives to build a tabbed pane view.

Implementing Draggable and Droppable Elements

In this example you will use custom AngularJS directives to implement a set of draggable elements containing words that can be dragged onto a set of droppable image elements. When the word is dropped on an image, it is appended to a list of words that appear below the image.

The purpose of this exercise is to show you an example of using the HTML5 drag and drop events. The example only uses the events, and the actual drag and drop functionality is built using the AngularJS mechanisms. The reason for this is to illustrate using AngularJS (plus, frankly, the HTML5 drag and drop is not well implemented and needs to be revised). Another thing illustrated in this example is appending new elements to existing ones in an AngularJS directive.

The folder structure for this example is as follows:

- **./server.js**: Node.js web server that serves the static project files.

- **./images**: Folder that contains the images used in the examples.

- **./ch11**: Project folder.

- **./ch11/dragdrop.html**: AngularJS template for the project.

- **./ch11/js/dragdrop.js**: AngularJS application supporting the custom drag and drop directives.

The code in Listing 11.5 contains the dragdrop.js application that defines two new custom AngularJS directives, dragit and dropit. Notice that in the parent scope the dragStatus and dropStatus variables are defined; these are updated in the custom directives. This is possible because no isolate scope is defined in the directives, so they share the parent controller scope.

Notice that inside the dragit directive the HTML5 draggable attribute is added to the dragit element using the attr() method. Also in the dragit directive the dragstart, drag, and dragend event handlers are implemented. For dragstart and drag, the default behavior is to allow the drag to start and dragenter/dragleave events to fire. However, dragend does prevent the default behavior so that our custom AngularJS code can handle the drop.

Inside the dropit directive, the dragover, dragleave, dragenter, and drop are implemented. Notice that in drop we use the append method to append a <p> element to the dropit element. The value inside the paragraph comes from the scope and was set during dragstart in the dragit directive. Once again, this is possible because no isolate scopes are defined in the directives.

Listing 11.5 **dragdrop.js: AngularJS Application That Implements dragit and dropit Custom AngularJS Directives to Provide Drag and Drop Functionality**

```
01 var app = angular.module('myApp', []);
02 app.controller('myController', function($scope) {
03     $scope.dragStatus = "none";
04     $scope.dropStatus = "none";
```

```
05   $scope.dropValue = "";
06 })
07 .directive('dragit', function($document, $window) {
08   function makeDraggable(scope, element, attr) {
09     angular.element(element).attr("draggable", "true");
10     element.on('dragstart', function(event) {
11       element.addClass('dragItem');
12       scope.$apply(function(){
13         scope.dragStatus = "Dragging " + element.html();
14         scope.dropValue = element.html();
15       });
16       event.dataTransfer.setData('Text', element.html());
17     });
18     element.on('drag', function(event) {
19       scope.$apply(function(){
20         scope.dragStatus = "X: " + event.pageX +
21                            " Y: " + event.pageY;
22       });
23     });
24     element.on('dragend', function(event) {
25       event.preventDefault();
26       element.removeClass('dragItem');
27     });
28   }
29   return {
30     link: makeDraggable
31   };
32 })
33 .directive('dropit', function($document, $window) {
34   return {
35     restrict: 'E',
36     link: function makeDroppable(scope, element, attr){
37       element.on('dragover', function(event) {
38         event.preventDefault();
39         scope.$apply(function(){
40           scope.dropStatus = "Drag Over";
41         });
42       });
43       element.on('dragleave', function(event) {
44         event.preventDefault();
45         element.removeClass('dropItem');
46         scope.$apply(function(){
47           scope.dropStatus = "Drag Leave";
48         });
49       });
50       element.on('dragenter', function(event) {
51         event.preventDefault();
```

```
52          element.addClass('dropItem');
53          scope.$apply(function(){
54            scope.dropStatus = "Drag Enter";
55          });
56        });
57        element.on('drop', function(event) {
58          event.preventDefault();
59          element.removeClass('dropItem');
60          scope.$apply(function(){
61            element.append('<p>' +
62                event.dataTransfer.getData('Text') + '</p>');
63            scope.dropStatus = "Dropped " + scope.dropValue;
64          });
65        });
66      }
67    };
68  });
```

The code in Listing 11.6 implements the AngularJS template that displays the dragStatus and dropStatus values. Notice that the draggable elements are declared using the <dragit> syntax and the droppable elements are declared using the <dropit> syntax.

Figure 11.2 shows the working AngularJS application in action. As words are dragged and dropped onto the images, they are appended below the image. Also notice that the drag coordinates and drop status are displayed as well.

Listing 11.6 **dragdrop.html: AngularJS Template That Uses the dragit and dropit Directives to Add Draggable and Droppable Elements to the Web Page**

```
01  <!doctype html>
02  <html ng-app="myApp">
03  <head>
04    <title>HTML5 Draggable and Droppable Directives</title>
05    <style>
06    dropit, img, p{
07      vertical-align: top; text-align: center;
08          width: 100px;
09          display: inline-block;
10          }
11        p {
12          color: white; background-color: black;
13          font: bold 14px/16px arial;
14      margin: 0px; width: 96px;
15      border: 2px ridge grey;
16      background: linear-gradient(#888888, #000000);
17          }
18          span{
```

```
19                display:inline-block; width: 100px;
20                font: 16px/18px Georgia, serif; text-align: center;
21                padding: 2px;
22                background: linear-gradient(#FFFFFF, #888888);
23              }
24            .dragItem {
25              color: red;
26          opacity: .5;
27              }
28        .dropItem {
29          border: 3px solid red;
30          opacity: .5;
31        }
32        #dragItems {
33          width: 400px;
34        }
35    </style>
36  </head>
37  <body>
38    <h2>HTML5 Drag and Drop Components</h2>
39    <div ng-controller="myController">
40      Drag Status: {{dragStatus}}<br>
41      Drop Status: {{dropStatus}}
42      <hr>
43      <div id="dragItems">
44          <span dragit>Nature</span>
45          <span dragit>Landscape</span>
46          <span dragit>Flora</span>
47          <span dragit>Sunset</span>
48          <span dragit>Arch</span>
49          <span dragit>Beauty</span>
50          <span dragit>Inspiring</span>
51        <span dragit>Summer</span>
52        <span dragit>Fun</span>
53      </div>
54      <hr>
55      <dropit><img src="/images/arch.jpg" /></dropit>
56      <dropit><img src="/images/flower.jpg" /></dropit>
57      <dropit><img src="/images/cliff.jpg" /></dropit>
58      <dropit><img src="/images/jump.jpg" /></dropit>
59    </div>
60    <script src="http://code.angularjs.org/1.3.0/angular.min.js"></script>
61    <script src="js/dragdrop.js"></script>
62  </body>
63  </html>
```

Figure 11.2   Using custom AngularJS directives to provide drag and drop functionality in a web page.

Adding a Zoom View Field to Images

In this example you will use a custom AngularJS directive to replace the `<img>` element and provide an automatic zoom view field that is displayed next to the image on the page. When you click on the image, the zoom view field will be updated with a zoomed-in portion of the image.

The purpose of this exercise is to show you how AngularJS custom directives can extend HTML with new elements that have a rich set of features. This example also illustrates another time when you will want to use the full version of jQuery rather than jQuery lite to get the size of the image and position of the mouse within the image.

The folder structure for this example is as follows:

- **./server.js**: Node.js web server that serves the static project files.
- **./images**: Folder that contains the images used in the examples.
- **./ch11**: Project folder.
- **./ch11/zooming.html**: AngularJS template for the project.
- **./ch11/zoomit.html**: AngularJS partial template that contains the image and zoom view field element definitions.
- **./ch11/js/zooming.js**: AngularJS application supporting the custom tabs directives.

The code in Listing 11.7 implements the `zooming.js` AngularJS application that defines the custom AngularJS directive called `zoomit`. The `zoomit` directive is restricted to elements only using `restrict: 'E'`. Also note that the `src` attribute from the template definition is injected into the `scope`.

The functionality for the `zoomit` directive is in the `controller` function. Notice that an object is created called `zInfo` that contains the `background-image` and `background-position` properties. The `zInfo` scope value will be used to set the `ng-style` attribute for the zoom view field in the `zoomit.html` partial template in Listing 11.8. Setting the `background-image` and `background-position` attributes adds the image to the background and positions the zoom.

The `imageClick()` function suppresses the default click behavior and then gets the `event.target` element as a jQuery object. This is where we need the full version of jQuery to the `height`, `width`, and current `offset` of the image on the page. We can then calculate the percentage from the left as `posX` and from the top as `posY` of the mouse click and set the `background-position` style appropriately.

Listing 11.7 `zooming.js`: AngularJS Application That Defines a Custom AngularJS Directive Called `zoomit` That Implements an `<img>` Element with a Zoom View Field

```
01 angular.module('myApp', [])
02 .controller('myController', ['$scope', function($scope) {
03 }])
04 .directive('zoomit', function() {
05   return {
06     restrict: 'E',
07     scope: { src: '@'},
08     controller: function($scope) {
09         $scope.zInfo = {
10             "background-image": "url(" + $scope.src + ")",
11             "background-position": "top right"
12         };
13         $scope.imageClick= function(event){
14           event.preventDefault();
15           //Using full jQuery to get offset, width and height
16           var elem = angular.element(event.target);
17           var posX = Math.ceil((event.pageX - elem.offset().left) /
18                               elem.width() * 100);
19           var posY = Math.ceil((event.pageY - elem.offset().top) /
20                               elem.height() * 100);
21           $scope.pos = posX + "% " + posY + "%";
22           $scope.zInfo["background-position"] = posX + "% " +
23                                               posY + "%";
24         };
25       },
26     link: function(scope, element, attrs) {
```

```
27        },
28      templateUrl: 'zoomit.html'
29    };
30 });
```

The code in Listing 11.8 implements the zoomit.html partial template that adds the <img>
element and a <div> element, which will have the zoomed image as a background. Notice that
the ng-click method is set to the imageClick() function in the scope and passes the $event.
Also notice that ng-style is set to zInfo in the scope.

**Listing 11.8   zoomit.html: AngularJS Partial Template That Implements the <img> and
<div> Elements for the Image and Zoom View Field**

```
01 <div>
02   <img src="{{src}}"
03        ng-click="imageClick($event)"/>
04   <div class="zoombox"
05        ng-style="zInfo"></div>
06 </div>
```

Listing 11.9 contains the AngularJS template code that provides the styles for the zoom view
field and image. Notice that the <zoomit> element is added just like any other and that the
src attribute is set just as with an <img> element. Also note that the full jQuery library is
loaded before the AngularJS library.

Figure 11.3 shows the images with their view fields on a web page. As you click on a particular
point in the image, the zoom view field is updated.

**Listing 11.9   zooming.html: AngularJS Template That Styles and Implements the
<zoomit> Custom AngularJS Directive**

```
01 <!DOCTYPE html>
02 <html  ng-app="myApp">
03   <head>
04     <title>Magnify</title>
05     <style>
06       .zoombox {
07         display: inline-block;
08         border: 3px ridge black;
09         width: 100px; height: 100px; }
10       img {
11         height: 200px;
12         vertical-align: top; }
13     </style>
14   </head>
15   <body>
```

```
16    <h2>Image Zoom Window</h2>
17    <div ng-controller="myController">
18      <zoomit   src="/images/flower.jpg"></zoomit>
19      <hr>
20      <zoomit   src="/images/arch.jpg"></zoomit>
21    </div>
22    </body>
23    <script
➥src="http://ajax.googleapis.com/ajax/libs/jquery/1.11.1/jquery.min.js"></script>
24    <script src="http://code.angularjs.org/1.3.0/angular.min.js"></script>
25    <script src="js/zooming.js"></script>
26    </html>
```

Figure 11.3   Implementing a custom AngularJS directive that provides an image with a zoom view finder.

Implementing Expandable and Collapsible Elements

In this example you will use custom AngularJS directives to build elements on the web page that can expand and contract. Each element will have a title and an expand/collapse button on top. When the collapse button is clicked, the contents of the element will be hidden. When the expand button is clicked, the contents will be shown again.

The purpose of this exercise is to solidify implementing custom AngularJS directives that nest inside each other and communicate with each other. In this example you also get to see how a scope gets isolated from the controller but shared between the expand container and the items in the container.

The folder structure for this example is as follows:

- **./server.js**: Node.js web server that serves the static project files.

- **./images**: Folder that contains the images used in the examples.

- **./ch11**: Project folder.

- **./ch11/expand.html**: AngularJS template for the project that implements the custom expandable directives.

- **./ch11/expand_list.html**: AngularJS partial template for the expandable element directive.

- **./ch11/expand_item.html**: AngularJS partial template for each individual item in the expandable element.

- **./ch11/js/expand.js**: AngularJS application supporting the expandable element directives.

The code in Listing 11.10 contains the expand.js AngularJS application that defines the expandList and expandItem custom AngularJS directives. The transclude option is used to keep the contents that get defined in the template.

Note that in the expandList directive, the scope is an isolate but accepts the attributes title and exwidth, which are set to title and listWidth in the scope. Note that in line 27 the listWidth value is used to set the width of the style for items added to the expand list. Also listWidth is used in line 34 to set the css attribute width for the expandable list.

The expandItem directive requires the expandList directive to provide access to the addItem() function tin the expandList directive's scope. Note that the myStyle attribute is used to build a style object that will be set to the ng-style for the item in the expanded list.

The way that expanding and collapsing work is that the myHide value is bound to each item in the expanded list using ng-hide in the template shown in Listing 11.11. The items property in the scope of expandList provides a list of scopes for each of the expandItem elements that get added. Then when the expand/collapse button is clicked, it is a simple matter of setting the myHide value to true or false in the scope for each item in the collapse() function to show or hide the items in the expanded element.

Listing 11.10 expand.js: AngularJS Application That Implements the expandList and expandItem Custom Directive to Provide Expandable and Collapsible Elements

```
01 angular.module('myApp', [])
02 .controller('myController', ['$scope', function($scope) {
03   $scope.items = [1,2,3,4,5];
04 }])
05 .directive('expandList', function() {
06   return {
07     restrict: 'E',
08     transclude: true,
09     scope: {title: '@', listWidth: '@exwidth'},
10     controller: function($scope) {
11       $scope.collapsed = false;
12       $scope.expandHandle = "-";
13       items = $scope.items = [];
14       $scope.collapse = function() {
15         if ($scope.collapsed){
16           $scope.collapsed = false;
17           $scope.expandHandle = "-";
18         } else {
19           $scope.collapsed = true;
20           $scope.expandHandle = "+";
21         }
22         angular.forEach($scope.items, function(item) {
23           item.myHide = $scope.collapsed;
24         });
25       };
26       this.addItem = function(item) {
27         item.myStyle.width = $scope.listWidth;
28         items.push(item);
29         item.myHide=false;
30       };
31     },
32     link: function(scope, element, attrs, expandCtrl) {
33       element.css("display", "inline-block");
34       element.css("width", scope.listWidth);
35     },
36     templateUrl: 'expand_list.html',
37   };
38 })
39 .directive('expandItem', function() {
40   return {
41     require: '^expandList',
42     restrict: 'E',
43     transclude: true,
44     scope: {},
```

```
45      controller: function($scope){
46          $scope.myHide = false;
47          $scope.myStyle = { width: "100px", "display": "inline-block" };
48          },
49      link: function(scope, element, attrs, expandCtrl) {
50          expandCtrl.addItem(scope);
51          },
52      templateUrl: 'expand_item.html',
53   };
54 });
```

Listing 11.11 contains the AngularJS partial template `expand_list.html` that provides the definition for the `expandList` element. The elements for the expand list header, including the expand/collapse button and the title, are added. The `<div ng-transclude>` element is where the `expandItem` elements will be placed.

Listing 11.11 `expand_list.html`: AngularJS Partial Template That Defines the `expandList` Element

```
01 <div>
02      <div class="expand-header">
03          <span class="expand-button"
04              ng-click="collapse()">{{expandHandle}}</span>
05          {{title}}
06      </div>
07      <div ng-transclude></div>
08 </div>
```

Listing 11.12 contains the AngularJS partial template `expand_item.html` that provides the definition for the expandable items. Notice that `ng-hide` is set to `myHide` in the scope to expand/collapse the element. `ng-style` is set to `myStyle` so that we can set the width to the expand list width. The `expand-item` class enables us to easily change the item appearance using CSS. The `ng-transclude` is used to place the contents from the AngularJS template definition inside the list item.

Listing 11.12 `expand_item.html`: AngularJS Partial Template That Defines the `expandItem` Element

```
01 <div ng-hide="myHide"
02      ng-style="myStyle"
03      class="expand-item"
04      ng-transclude>
05 </div>
```

Listing 11.13 implements the AngularJS template that provides the styles for the page as well as definitions for the <expand-list> elements. Notice that four different <expand-list> elements are defined. The first is a simple list where the <expand-item> element contains just text. The next provides a single <expand-item> element with form elements. The third contains a mixture of different HTML elements in each <expand-item> element. The final one contains just an <img> element.

Note that each <expand-list> element contains a different value for the attributes title and exwidth, which results in lists with different titles and widths on the page. The results of the AngularJS application are shown in Figure 11.4. Notice the expanded and collapsed version of the elements.

Listing 11.13   **expand.html: AngularJS Code That Styles and Implements Expandable/ Collapsible Elements Using the expandList and expandItem Custom Directives**

```
01 <!DOCTYPE html>
02 <html  ng-app="myApp">
03   <head>
04    <title>Expandable and Collapsible Lists</title>
05    <style>
06      * { vertical-align: top; }
07      expand-list{
08        border: 2px ridge black; }
09      .expand-header{
10        text-align: center;
11        font: bold 16px/24px arial;
12         background-image: linear-gradient(#CCCCCC, #EEEEEE);
13         }
14      .expand-button{
15        float: left; padding: 2px 4px;
16        font: bold 22px/16px courier;
17        color: white; background-color: black;
18        cursor: pointer;
19        border: 3px groove grey; }
20      .expand-item {
21        border: 1px ridge black;}
22      p { margin: 0px; padding: 2px;}
23      label { display: inline-block; width: 80px; padding: 2px; }
24      .small { width: 100px; padding: 2px; }
25      .large { width: 300px; }
26    </style>
27   </head>
28   <body>
29   <h2>Expandable and Collapsible Lists</h2>
30   <hr>
31   <div ng-controller="myController">
32     <expand-list title="Companion" exwidth="120px">
```

```
33        <expand-item>Rose</expand-item>
34        <expand-item>Donna</expand-item>
35        <expand-item>Martha</expand-item>
36        <expand-item>Amy</expand-item>
37        <expand-item>Rory</expand-item>
38      </expand-list>
39      <expand-list title="Form" exwidth="280px">
40        <expand-item>
41          <label>Name</label>
42          <input type="text" /><br>
43          <label>Phone</label>
44          <input type="text" /><br>
45          <label>Address</label>
46          <input type="text" /><br>
47          <label>Comment</label>
48          <textarea type="text"></textarea>
49        </expand-item>
50      </expand-list>
51      <hr>
52      <expand-list title="Mixed List" exwidth="300px">
53        <expand-item>Text Item</expand-item>
54        <expand-item><p>I think therefore I am.</p></expand-item>
55        <expand-item>
56          <img class="small" src="/images/jump.jpg" />Sunset
57        </expand-item>
58        <expand-item>
59          <ul>
60            <li>AngularJS</li>
61            <li>jQuery</li>
62            <li>JavaScript</li>
63          </ul>
64        </expand-item>
65      </expand-list>
66      <expand-list title="Image" exwidth="300px">
67        <expand-item>
68          <img class="large" src="/images/lake.jpg" />
69        </expand-item>
70      </expand-list>
71    </div>
72    </body>
73    <script src="http://code.angularjs.org/1.3.0/angular.min.js"></script>
74    <script src="js/expand.js"></script>
75  </html>
```

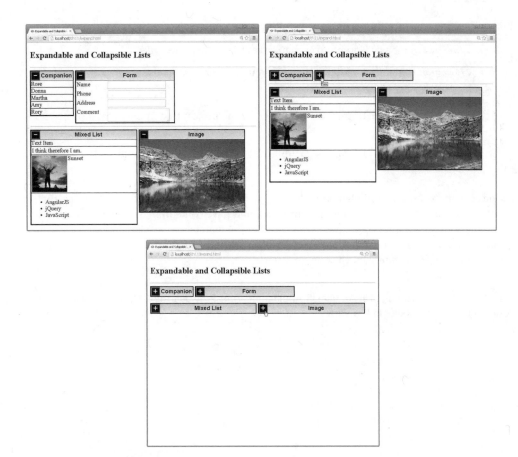

Figure 11.4   Using custom AngularJS directives to build and implement expandable/collapsible web page elements.

Adding Star Ratings to Elements

In this example you will use just the AngularJS scope, controller, and view to implement elements that implement the star ratings for images. When you click on a star, the rating changes in the scope and the number of stars changes.

The purpose of this exercise is just to remind you that much of the data binding and view interactions can be accomplished in basic AngularJS templates without the need for custom directives.

The folder structure for this example is as follows:

- **./server.js**: Node.js web server that serves the static project files.

- **./images**: Folder that contains the images used in the examples.

- **./ch11**: Project folder.

- **./ch11/rating.html**: AngularJS template for the project that implements a simple star rating to elements.

- **./ch11/js/rating.js**: AngularJS application that defines the supporting star rating elements.

The code in Listing 11.14 implements the rating.js AngularJS application. Notice that the data used comes from $scope.items. This data could have come from a service, a database or another source. The array $scope.stars is used in the template to display the stars on the web page. The only function required in the controller code is adjustRating, which is called when the user changes the rating by clicking on a star.

Listing 11.14   rating.js: AngularJS Application That Provides the Data and Functionality to Support Star Ratings in the View

```
01 angular.module('myApp', [])
02 .controller('myController', ['$scope', function($scope) {
03     $scope.stars = [1,2,3,4,5];
04     $scope.items = [
05         {
06             description: "Delicate Arch",
07             img: "/images/arch.jpg",
08             rating: 3},
09         {
10             description: "Silver Lake",
11             img: "/images/lake.jpg",
12             rating: 4},
13         {
14             description: "Yellowstone Bison",
15             img: "/images/bison.jpg",
16             rating: 4}
17     ];
18     $scope.adjustRating = function(item, value){
19         item.rating = value;
20     };
21 }]);
```

The code in Listing 11.15 implements an AngularJS template that iterates through the items array from the scope and builds out the image elements complete with the description and star rating. Note that to build the star list, ng-repeat is used on the stars array from the scope.

Also note in Line 31 that to set whether a star or an empty star is displayed, the `ng-class` attribute is set based on the item `rating` being greater than the star index. The `ng-click` attribute is used to bind mouse clicks on each star to the `adjustRating()` function in the scope to set the rating for this item.

The resulting web page is shown in Figure 11.5. Notice that as the stars are clicked, the rating and stars displayed also change.

Listing 11.15 `rating.html`: AngularJS Template That Utilizes Data from the Scope to Display a List of Images with Descriptions and Ratings

```
01  <!DOCTYPE html>
02  <html  ng-app="myApp">
03    <head>
04      <title>Ratings</title>
05      <style>
06        img {
07          width: 100px; }
08        .star {
09          display: inline-block;
10          width: 15px;
11          background-image: url("/images/star.png");
12          background-repeat: no-repeat;
13        }
14        .empty {
15          display: inline-block;
16          width: 15px;
17          background-image: url("/images/empty.png");
18          background-repeat: no-repeat;
19        }
20      </style>
21    </head>
22    <body>
23    <h2>Images With Ratings</h2>
24    <hr>
25    <div ng-controller="myController">
26      <div ng-repeat="item in items">
27        <img ng-src="{{item.img}}" />
28        {{item.description}}<br>
29        Rating: {{item.rating}} stars<br>
30        <span ng-repeat="idx in stars"
31            ng-class=
32              "{true: 'star', false: 'empty'}[idx <= item.rating]"
33            ng-click="adjustRating(item, idx)"> 
34      </span>
35      <hr>
36    </div>
```

```
37   </div>
38   </body>
39   <script src="http://code.angularjs.org/1.3.0/angular.min.js"></script>
40   <script src="js/rating.js"></script>
41  </html>
```

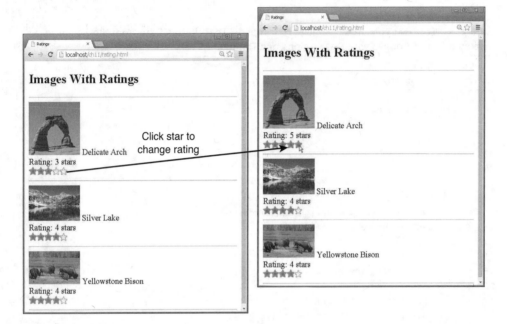

Figure 11.5   Implementing a simple star rating in elements using just AngularJS scope data,
controller code, and a template view.

Summary

AngularJS provides many tools to extend the capability of HTML through the use of templates
with built-in and custom directives. In this chapter you got several looks at different ways in
which you can implement richly interactive elements into your web pages in an easy yet structured way.

In this chapter you also got a look at several custom directives. The tabbed panels and expand-
able/collapsible examples showed different ways to implement directives that nest inside each
other and interact with each other. The drag and drop showed you one way to interact with
the HTML5 drag and drop events, as well as sharing the scope between the controller and
custom directives. The star rating example showed you how to build interactivity using only

the AngularJS scope, controller, and template. The zoom view field example showed you how to extend the concept of an HTML `<img>` element to an element that includes an additional zoom element that interacts with mouse clicks in the image.

That's a wrap for this book. I hope that you have enjoyed learning about AngularJS as much as I have. I love AngularJS because it makes it easy to write structured code without a lot of complexity. With AngularJS everything has its place as a view, directive, controller, service, or part of the data model. After reading this book, you should have a good understanding of the AngularJS framework so that you feel confident in jumping in and writing your own AngularJS applications. Enjoy your coding!

Appendix A

Testing AngularJS Applications

An important part, if not the most important part, of any AngularJS project is testing. Good testing provides you with the freedom to modify, adapt, and grow your AngularJS applications without major complications and problems. There are several types of testing that I've heard about through the years. For this appendix I want to talk only about unit testing and end-to-end testing and how they relate to AngularJS.

This appendix is designed as more of an informational introduction to testing AngularJS applications. For the most part, the appendix discusses concepts with a few examples and then points you to some locations where you can get additional information. The reason for this is that there is no single way to test AngularJS applications. Your testing strategy should be based on your environment, your skill set, your budget, and the specific needs of your application.

Deciding on a Testing Platform

There are several different platforms you can use for testing JavaScript applications. Which one you go with might depend on what your engineers are most familiar with, what your budget is, which JavaScript framework you need, or just what you are already using.

These are all very real and important concerns, and you will need to make your decision based on them. That being said, the AngularJS group seems to have gravitated toward Jasmine as their unit test framework. It makes sense. Jasmine is the kind of framework that seems to provide a lot of functionality while not getting in the way of testing. In fact, for end-to-end testing you will need to use Protractor, which uses the Jasmine syntax for testing.

You should take some time to evaluate the framework you decide on, because you will likely be using it for a while. You can get a list of the more well-known JavaScript testing frameworks at Wikipedia: http://en.wikipedia.org/wiki/List_of_unit_testing_frameworks#JavaScript.

After you decide on a testing platform, you will need to understand how to implement the various testing concepts, such as pretest buildup work, post-test teardown, and mock objects and services, for the rest of this appendix to make much sense.

Understanding AngularJS Unit Tests

Unit testing AngularJS applications is very similar to unit testing other frameworks. I'm not going to go into the details of unit testing in this appendix since it is framework specific. Rather, I am going to discuss some aspects of unit testing and how they apply to AngularJS mechanisms.

A lot of the information I am providing here can also be found in the AngularJS documentation. I've added the URL to the AngularJS unit testing documentation here to provide some additional thoughts:

> https://docs.angularjs.org/guide/unit-testing

Dependencies and Unit Tests

Dependencies are one of the most widely used mechanisms in AngularJS. You see them everywhere, from dependency injection to global services. This can present a problem when it comes to unit tests because you don't really want to have to test the full functionality of the dependency within the unit test. Instead, you will want to get the dependency and control it with your own mock objects and services.

There are four methods for controlling the dependency injection:

- Create your own instance of the dependency using the `new` operator.
- Create the dependency as a global object you can look up anywhere.
- Ask a registry for it. This option requires that you have access to the registry as well, which means also placing it in a global location.
- Have the dependency passed to you.

The following sections describe each of these methods in AngularJS.

Using the `new` Operator

Consider the following function and assume that `MyService` is a global service that you can create an instance of:

```
function MyClass() {
  this.doSomething = function() {
    var gSrv = new MyService();
    var data = sSrv.getSomething();
  }
}
```

To control `MyService` you would need to do something like this:

```
var savedMyService = MyService;
MyService = function MockMyService() {};
```

```
var myClass = new MyClass();
myClass.doSomething();
MyService = savedMyService;
```

This works; however, you run the risk of losing the handle to `MyService` if things go wrong, so you need to be careful.

Using a Global Lookup

This is similar to using the `new` operator. Consider the following function and assume that `global.myService` is a singleton instance of the `MyService` service you need:

```
function MyClass() {
  this.doSomething = function() {
    var data = global.myService.getSomething();
  }
}
```

To control `MyService` you would need to do something like this:

```
var savedMyService = global.myService;
global.myService = function MockMyService() {};
var myClass = new MyClass();
myClass.doSomething();
global.myService = savedMyService;
```

Again, this works, but because you run the risk of losing the handle to `global.myService` if things go wrong, you need to be careful.

Requesting the Dependency from a Registry

Consider the following function and assume that `global.serviceRegistry` is a singleton instance of a registry that has the `MyService` service registered:

```
function MyClass() {
  this.doSomething = function() {
    var myService = global.serviceRegistry.get('MyService');
    var data = myService.getSomething();
  }
}
```

To control `MyService` you would need to do something like this:

```
var savedRegistry = global.serviceRegistry;
//create new globel.serviceRegistry
global.serviceRegistry.set('MyService', function MockMyService() {});
var myClass = new MyClass();
myClass.doSomething();
global.serviceRegistry = savedRegistry;
```

Again, this works, but because you run the risk of losing the handle to `global.service-Registry` if things go wrong, you need to be careful.

Passing the Dependency as a Parameter

I showed you the first three methods so that when you see the passed parameter method you will recognize that this is really the way you should be doing it. You should try to design your dependency usage such that the dependency can be passed in to the consumer. That way you can easily control the dependency from the test.

Now, consider the following function and assume that `myService` is an instance of a service that is typically passed in:

```
function MyClass() {
  this.doSomething = function(myService) {
    var data = myService.getSomething();
  }
}
```

To control `MyService` all you need to do is the following:

```
var mockedService = function MockMyService() {};
var myClass = new MyClass();
myClass.doSomething(mockedService);
```

Testing Controllers with User Input Bound to Scope Data

AngularJS makes it very simple to test HTML elements that are bound to the scope of the controller. This is because the values are stored in scope and can directly be referenced in the controller.

Consider a web page that has a single text `<input>` element that you have a back-end function to test, and verify that it is not empty and that it is fewer than 10 characters.

```
<body>
  Data: <input type="text" />
</body>
```

The back-end code would look something like this:

```
function InputCtrl(){
  var input = $('input');
  var val = input.val();
  this.verify = function(){
    if (val.length > 0 $$ val.length < 10){
      return true;
    } else {
      return false;
    };
  }
}
```

To test this you would need to actually create the input element and inject it into the web page similar to the following:

```
var input = $('<input type="text"/>');
$('body').html('<div>')
  .find('div')
    .append(input);
var pc = new InputCtrl();
input.val('abc');
var result = pc.verify ();
expect(result).toEqual(true);
$('body').empty();
```

If you think about it, this can get extremely messy the more inputs that are involved. In AngularJS if the value of the input is bound to the scope, it is much simpler. The following shows the AngularJS controller definition, in which the value of the text input is bound to `$scope.inStr`:

```
function InputCtrl($scope){
  $scope.inStr = '';
  $scope.verify = function(){
    if ($scope.inStr.length > 0 $$ $scope.inStr.length < 10){
      return true;
    } else {
      return false;
    };
  }
}
```

Now the test can look something like the following:

```
var $scope = {};
var mc = $controller('InputCtrl', { $scope: $scope });
$scope.inStr = 'abc';
var result = $scope.verify();
expect(result).toEqual(true);
```

You should see the value of binding input values to scope variables in the controller whenever possible.

Testing Filters

Testing your custom filters in AngularJS can be very simple if you keep them straightforward. To illustrate this, consider the following custom filter and test:

```
myModule.filter('nospace', function() {
  return function(text){
    return text.replace(' ', '');
  }
```

```
});
var nospace = $filter('nospace');
expect(nospace('my words')).toEqual('mywords');
```

Testing Simple Directives

It is important to test your custom directives in AngularJS due to the complexity of encapsulating functionality within custom HTML tags, attributes, classes, or comments. Unit tests are the best way to do this because they can cover the variety of ways the custom element can be used.

For simple directives you will need to use the $compile method to compile the object first and then the $digest() method to fire off all watches in the scope to ensure that expressions are evaluated. Also, if you are running multiple tests, you should create the module and inject the $compile and $rootScope into each test using a pretest buildup method.

To illustrate this, consider the following custom directive two-plus-two in a template:

```
<two-plus-two></two-plus-two>
```

The controller code for the directive is shown here:

```
var app = angular.module('myApp', []);
app.directive('twoPlusTwo', function () {
    return {
        restrict: 'E',
        replace: true,
        template: '<h1>Two Plus Two is {{ 2 + 2 }} </h1>'
    };
});
```

To illustrate testing the controller, I needed to pick a testing framework. The following shows an example of a Jasmine test to test the functionality of the custom directive. Notice how the myApp module, $compile, and $rootScope are injected into every test using beforeEach() and that $compile and $digest are used to compile and render the element and evaluate the expression.

```
describe('Unit testing addition', function() {
  var $compile;
  var $rootScope;
  beforeEach(module('myApp'));
  beforeEach(inject(function(_$compile_, _$rootScope_){
    $compile = _$compile_;
    $rootScope = _$rootScope_;
  }));
  it('Adds element and handles filter', function() {
    var element = $compile("<two-plus-two></two-plus-two>")($rootScope);
    $rootScope.$digest();
    expect(element.html()).toContain("Two Plus Two is 4");
  });
});
```

Testing Custom Directives That Use Transclusion

There are some additional things you need to know if you are testing custom AngularJS directives that include transclusion. Directives that use transclusion are treated specially by the compiler in that the contents of the directive's elements are removed and provided via a transclusion function before their compile function is called. Only then will the directive's template be appended to the directive's element. At that point it can then insert the transcluded content.

I know that's a lot to grasp, so here is how the process works when `transclude: true` is used. This is the element before compilation:

```
<div translude-directive>
  "transcluded content"
</div>
```

Here is what the element looks like after transclusion extraction:

```
<div transclude-directive></div>
```

Now after compilation:

```
<div transclude-directive>
  "template content"
  <span ng-transclude>"transcluded content"</span>
</div>
```

And here is how the process works if you are using `transclude: 'element'`. The compiler removes the directive's entire element from the DOM and replaces it with a comment node. Then the compiler appends the directive's template as a sibling to the comment node:

```
<div element-transclude>
  "transclude content"
</div>
```

After transclusion extraction:

```
<!-- elementTransclude -->
```

After compilation:

```
<!-- elementTransclude -->
<div element-transclude>
  "template content"
  <span ng-transclude>"transcluded content"</span>
</div>
```

The reason this needs to be pointed out is that you need to treat tests for directives that use `'element'` transclusion differently. When you define the directive on the root element of the DOM fragment, `$compile` will return the comment node and you will lose the ability to access the template and transcluded content. This is shown in the following test snippet:

```
var node = $compile('<div element-transclude></div>')($rootScope);
expect(node[0].nodeType).toEqual(node.COMMENT_NODE);
expect(node[1]).toBeUndefined();
```

The way to handle this is to make certain that you wrap your transcluded directive inside another element such as a `<div>` when you are using the `transclude: 'element'` parameters for the custom directive. For example:

```
var node = $compile('<div><div element-transclude></div></div>')($rootScope);
var contents = node.contents();
expect(contents[0].nodeType).toEqual(node.COMMENT_NODE);
expect(contents[1].nodeType).toEqual(node.ELEMENT_NODE);
```

Testing Directives that Use External Templates

The AngularJS folks kind of punt on this one a bit. Their suggestion, if you use a custom AngularJS directive that uses external templates via the `templateUrl` parameter, is to use something like `karma-ng-html2js-preprocessor` to precompile HTML templates and thus avoid having to load them over HTTP during tests.

You can get `karma-ng-html2js-preprocessor` here:

> https://github.com/karma-runner/karma-ng-html2js-preprocessor

Understanding AngularJS End-to-End Testing

I do like using end-to-end testing for web applications; however, in my opinion it is used much too often as the major (if not the only testing). End-to-end testing is great for verifying the system in a general way, but for AngularJS applications you should be using unit testing for the majority of your testing needs.

That having been said, you should also consider implementing some end-to-end testing that can catch regression issues and generally test the overall functionality of your system. End-to-end testing can also expose some system limitation problems such as network or database bandwidth.

The AngularJS folks have created a tool called Protractor that enables you to implement end-to-end testing of your AngularJS applications. Protractor is a Node.js program that will run end-to-end tests written in JavaScript. It uses WebDriver to control the browsers and simulate user actions. The language syntax for Protractor is based on Jasmine, so if you are familiar with Jasmine you should be able to come up to speed quickly.

The idea of end-to-end testing with Protractor is that you can set up certain things in the test environment using Jasmine code and then use WebDriver to provide input to the application through the web browser and then validate the results.

End-to-end testing will vary greatly based on environmental, design, technology, and other variables, so I'm not going to go into it in this appendix. However, I'd suggest going to the following links when you do decide to try implementing end-to-end programming in your AngularJS applications:

https://docs.angularjs.org/guide/e2e-testing

https://github.com/angular/protractor/blob/master/docs/getting-started.md

https://code.google.com/p/selenium/wiki/GettingStarted

Index

D

N

S

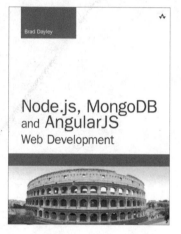